CAKES
for the boys

Helen Penman

13 themed cake designs for boys and men of all ages

dedication

To David and Charlie, my husband and youngest son, who have been a great support to me throughout the whole process of putting this book together.

First published in May 2012 by B. Dutton Publishing Limited, The Grange, Hones Yard, Farnham, Surrey, GU9 8BB.
Copyright: Helen Penman 2012
ISBN-13: 978-1-905113-33-0
All rights reserved.

Publisher: Beverley Dutton
Editor: Jenny Stewart
Art Director/Designer: Sarah Ryan
Deputy Editor: Jenny Royle
Designer: Zena Manicom
Sub Editor/Graphic Designer: Louise Pepé
Editorial Assistant: Amy Norman
PR and Advertising Manager: Natalie Bull
Photography: Alister Thorpe
Printed in Spain

introduction

Whilst I was writing my first cake carving book, *Squires Kitchen's Guide to Cake Shaping*, I came up with the idea of writing a book full of interesting cake designs for men and boys. I have often been asked for birthday or celebration cakes suitable for boys of all ages and realised that whilst there are novelty cake books for the usual assortment of sporting, gardening, sailing and children's cakes, I felt there was so much more to offer aspiring cake makers. I wanted to design cakes that would enthuse the reader to make spectacular creations that would amaze!

I have tried to include a wide range of designs in this book so that there is something for everyone, from little boys through to teenagers, adults and the young at heart! All of the cakes are carved into shape which makes them all different and unique, which I hope will inspire you to be really creative with your designs. Amongst the projects you will find car cakes which show you how to make any model of car without the fear that it won't be recognised, something I know us cake makers worry about!

I hope this book will show you that carving a cake isn't as daunting as you might think and the results can be truly rewarding. Even the cake crumbs can be baked into delicious treats to accompany the fantastic celebration cake that your guests will be admiring!

I hope you – and your sons, husbands, boyfriends, granddads, uncles and friends – have fun with the cakes in this book.

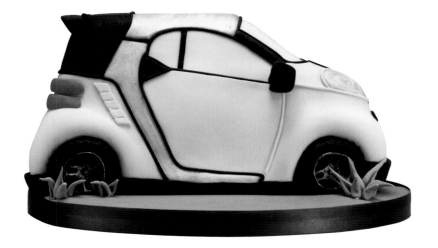

acknowledgements

I would like to thank my mother, Maureen, for making all the cakes for me, some at quite short notice.

Thanks also Beverley, Jenny, Sarah and Zena at Squires Kitchen for working so hard and keeping me on track and again putting together an amazing book, not forgetting Alister for the fantastic photography, showing my cakes at their best angle!

contents

PROJECTS

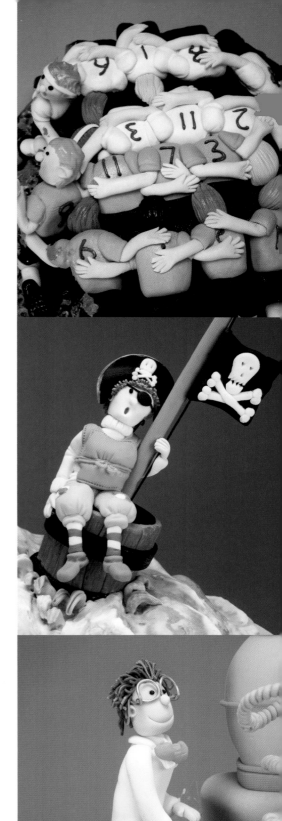

equipment

The basic equipment you need to make the cakes in this book is virtually the same throughout – any extra items are listed at the beginning of each project. Make sure you have all the basic equipment you need before you start and keep all your tools for sugarcraft use only. Suppliers for sugarcraft tools and equipment are listed on page 96.

1 Acetate sheets: an ideal material for making templates as they can be wiped clean and reused.

2 Aluminium foil: ideal for supporting pieces as they dry as it can be formed into any shape. To prevent the foil from marking large pieces of paste, cover with kitchen towel first.

3 Ball tool: the rounded ends of this tool make it perfect for indenting paste and for smoothing areas that are difficult to reach.

4 Cake dummies: polystyrene dummies are usually used to represent a cake where you are looking to achieve height but without the excess cake. They are also excellent as formers for drying paste as the piece will have the exact curvature as a cake of the same size.

5 Cake smoothers: I use these on every project I make, not always on the cake but always on the drum to smooth and polish the paste, removing grains of icing sugar and finger marks. A pad of paste also works well on areas of the cake that aren't flat and require something more flexible.

6 Cocktail sticks: use these for adding small amounts of concentrated food colour to sugarpaste and for holding templates in place on cakes (if you prefer not to use glass-headed pins, see overleaf).

7 Craft knife: ideal for cutting paste to give a sharp, accurate finish. Keep this for sugarcraft use only.

8 Cutters: a huge range of cutters is available from sugarcraft suppliers, including flowers and leaves, geometric shapes and animals. A set of round cutters is always handy to have in your kit box and any specific cutters that are used in the book are listed at the beginning of each project. If you don't have a particular cutter you can always make your own template from thin card or acetate and cut the shape from paste with a craft knife or cutting wheel.

9 Dowelling rods: these are made of food-grade plastic and provide internal support to cakes where needed. Sterilise them with clear spirit or boiling water before use. To dowel a cake, insert them into the covered cake, mark level with the

cake covering to the length you require, pull them out and lay flat on a cutting board. Using a craft knife, cut off the excess (if you cut through it part way, you can snap it off to the length required) and then re-insert into the cake.

10 Floral tape: I always have black floral tape in my kit box for binding wires together.

11 Floral wire: useful for making pieces that need to hold their shape (such as the Alien's arm). Never insert wires directly into any part of a cake that is to be eaten: always insert the wire into a posy pick filled with paste then push this into the cake. If wires are used on models (such as the Mad Professor), make sure this part is not eaten.

12 Flower shaping tool: this is the tool I would take with me if I was marooned on a desert island! I use it for nearly everything from marking creases to smoothing paste, attaching tiny dots of paste and so many other purposes.

13 Foam pad: used to soften thin pieces of paste such as petals. To thin, cup or frill a flower or petal, place it onto the foam and press firmly with a bone or ball tool.

14 Glass-headed pins: useful for holding templates in place whilst you cut around them, or to pin ribbon to the edge of a cake drum instead of using a glue stick or tape. Always use glass-headed pins so they can be seen and removed easily and never use pins on a finished cake as this would be dangerous. Always sterilise pins with clear spirit or boiling water before using with food.

15 Greaseproof paper: ideal for making templates, tracings, piping bags, and for lining cake tins.

16 Heated craft pen: not essential but a handy tool for making your own acetate stencils if you can't find a pre-cut one that suits your design.

17 Kitchen roll: useful for blotting excess dust from paintbrushes before dusting cakes and for supporting pieces while they are drying.

18 Mini palette knife (or Kemper tool): a useful tool for carving fine detail into cakes, for picking up and trimming fine sugar pieces and for applying buttercream to hard-to-reach places.

19 Non-slip mat: place under the work

board to prevent it from moving as you work, and use in cake boxes and under boxes when you are transporting cakes from one place to another.

20 Craft mat: if you are making your own acetate templates using a heated craft pen, make sure you use a heatproof mat underneath.

21 Non-stick boards, large and small: green acrylic boards are always useful for rolling out pastes as they protect the work surface and can be cleaned and put away easily.

22 Paintbrushes: you will find it helpful to have a selection of brushes to hand including fine, pointed brushes for painting and gluing and large, flat brushes for dusting. Good quality brushes are available from sugarcraft suppliers (see page 96).

23 Palette knives: a small, cranked palette knife can be used to pick up sugar pieces easily and also for spreading buttercream onto cakes. You may also find a large, straight palette knife useful for filling cakes.

24 Sharp knives: use a large, serrated knife for cutting layers in cakes and a

smaller paring knife for trimming and shaping.

25 Piping bags: you can make your own piping bags from greaseproof paper or you can buy them readymade. Plastic piping bags are also available, and you can choose from disposable and re-useable. These are particularly good for use with the larger nozzles that require larger quantities of filling, such as cream.

26 Piping nozzles (tubes): nos. 1 and 1.5 nozzles are used to decorate several of the cakes in this book. They can be used to write inscriptions or to add fine details to cake work.

27 Pizza wheel (not pictured): useful for cutting out large pieces of sugarpaste neatly and cleanly.

28 Posy pick (not pictured): this is inserted into the cake to hold wires or similar decorations that must not come directly into contact with the cake. Fill the pick with sugarpaste, then push in the wires so they are held securely. Finally, push the pick into the cake so that it is flush with the surface. Make sure the recipient is aware that the posy pick is in the cake so that it can be removed safely.

29 Raw spaghetti: I often use this to add internal support to items, such as a head on a figure. Remember to remove any spaghetti strands before the cake is eaten.

30 Ribbon cutter: if you're making sugar ribbons, bands or strips this tool is very useful for cutting long, even strips of paste.

31 Rolling pins, large and small: use straight, acrylic rolling pins as they give a smooth finish to sugarpaste, flower paste, modelling paste and marzipan. Use the large one for covering cakes and the small one for decoration.

32 Ruler: this is always useful for making sure your cakes are the right size, particularly when making car templates (such as in the Microcar and Camper Van projects).

33 Scissors: useful for cutting paste, ribbon and card for templates. Keep a pair of fine scissors solely for sugarcraft use.

34 Side marker: a useful tool for scribing lines around the side of a cake at a given height so you can then cut the cake accurately before filling (see pages 21 to 22).

35 Sieve: whilst this is used to sieve dry ingredients for baking, I often use it to texture paste and make grass by pushing green paste through the mesh.

36 Spare cake drums: useful when you are making lots of small decorations that need to be kept to one side or for sliding the top slice of cake onto when filling a cake.

37 Stitching wheel (quilting tool): this has a veining tool at one end and a wheel at the other that indents a stitched effect on paste.

38 Sugar shaper: this versatile tool has different discs that can be inserted in the end to form softened sugarpaste or flower paste into different shapes and sizes for decoration. I find the single-hole 'string' disc is one of the most useful.

39 Texture mats: designed to emboss a pattern onto soft paste, these add detail in a very quick and easy way.

40 Veining/frilling tool: one end is ideal for marking smiles on figures, whilst the other end can be used for marking veins on petals and leaves.

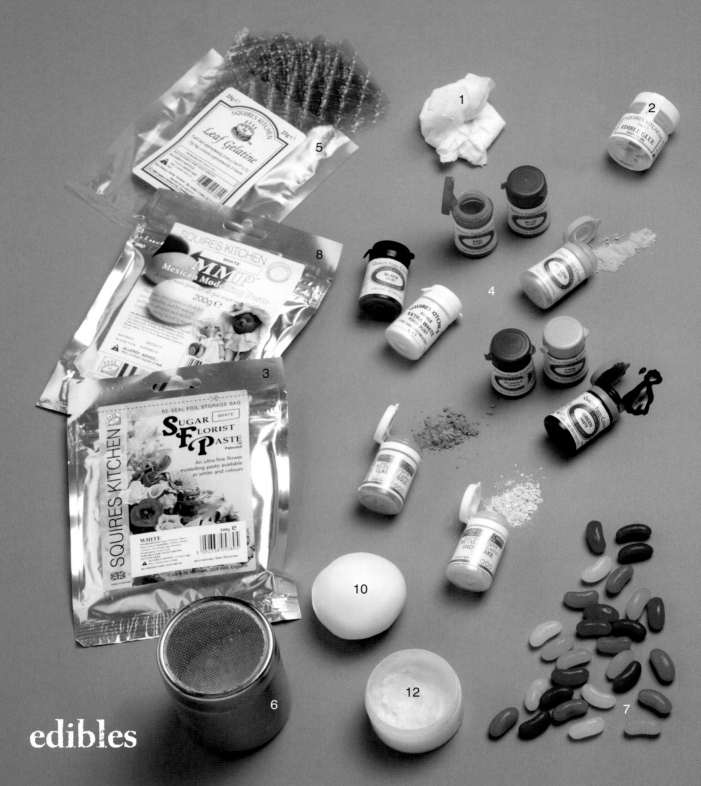

edibles

There are several edible items that you will need for virtually every cake you make, and others that are useful to have for particular projects. The edibles pictured here show everything that is used to decorate the cakes throughout the book, but I have also included specific colours and quantities with each project so you can make sure you have everything to hand before you start.

1 Cornflour duster: use a light dusting of cornflour when rolling out flower paste to prevent it from sticking. To make a cornflour duster, place a spoonful of cornflour in the centre of a muslin square and tie the corners with an elastic band.

2 Edible glue: this is needed to glue sugar items together. Brush a little glue onto the surface of the piece, hold it in place for a few moments then support with crumpled kitchen towel until the glue has dried. Edible glue can be bought readymade from Squires Kitchen (see page 96) or made using a small amount of white modelling paste mixed with pre-boiled water. The homemade glue can be thinned down by adding more pre-boiled water (always use boiled water to ensure there are no bacteria present). A little gum arabic mixed with cooled, boiled water is another good alternative to readymade edible glue.

3 Flower paste (Sugar Florist Paste/ gum paste): a paste that is normally used to make sugar flowers and leaves as it can be rolled very finely without tearing. In novelty work it is ideal for pieces that need to hold their shape as it dries quickly and very hard. It can also be added to sugarpaste to give it more stretch.

4 Food colourings: these are available as pastes, liquids and dusts. When colouring sugarpaste, flower paste and other roll-out pastes I prefer to use paste colours rather than liquids because they don't change the consistency of the medium being coloured. Always add colour in small amounts using a cocktail stick – remember that you can add more but you can't take it out. Dust colours (powders) are applied to the surface of sugar pieces – they are excellent for adding a colour to a finished item, to give shade and depth with a complementary colour or to add a contrasting colour to a small area. Ranges of dust colours are available with different effects such as metallics, sparkles or lustres.

5 Gelatine: this is usually used for setting jellies but when it comes in leaves (sheets) it looks like glass and can be used on cakes as an edible item. Remember, however, that it is not suitable for vegetarians.

6 Icing sugar: a shaker with fine holes is perfect for dusting work surfaces to prevent sugarpaste from sticking.

7 Jellybeans: if you are making cakes or cupcakes for children, sweets are a quick and easy decoration. They can also be incorporated into novelty cake designs such as the Mad Professor (see page 64).

8 Mexican Modelling Paste (SK): a readymade paste that is ideal to use in moulds (as it is non-sticky), for modelling (as it holds its shape), and it can be folded, veined and creased with great results. Sometimes if a more supportive paste is needed, a little gum tragacanth can be added. The paste does need some support while drying but once dry it stays firm whilst remaining soft enough to cut and eat.

9 Royal icing (not pictured): this is often used to stick decorations in place and to pipe details or inscriptions onto cakes. You can either make your own (see recipe on page 17) or use Squires Kitchen's Instant Mix Royal Icing where you just need to add water.

10 Sugarpaste (rolled fondant): usually used for the outer covering on novelty cakes as it is soft and pliable, sugarpaste can be folded, indented and creased, and it can also be smoothed flat. I generally use white sugarpaste and colour it with paste colours, except where a very strong colour such as black is used – I always buy this ready coloured as it can get quite messy otherwise!

11 Vodka (or any colourless spirit, not pictured): this is used to thin out paste colours for painting or to make paint from dusting powders. It leaves no taste and evaporates rapidly so the colours won't run when dry. If you would rather not use alcohol you can use a little pre-boiled water instead.

12 White vegetable fat: you will need to add a little white vegetable fat to paste when used with a sugar shaper to make it easier to extrude. A little of this on your hands will also help to soften up flower paste if it has dried out and can be used to stop paste from sticking to the board and rolling pin instead of icing sugar.

hints and tips for baking

Whether you bake regularly or only on special occasions, here are a few tips that will help you achieve a perfect cake every time.

Follow the ingredient measurements carefully and stick to either metric or imperial throughout.

Allow your oven to get up to temperature before you put your cake in to make sure it bakes evenly.

Always line your cake tins with greaseproof paper: full instructions are given opposite.

Creaming butter and sugar requires vigorous beating to aerate the mixture, making it soft and fluffy. This can be done by hand but is quicker in a food mixer or processor if you have one. It is also much easier to achieve if the butter is soft: if you forget to get it out of the fridge, give it a blast in the microwave for 10 seconds.

I find that butter is much better than margarine as it has a finer flavour and, unlike oil, it can be beaten to incorporate air. Unsalted is best for cakes, although shortbread is heavenly when made with salted butter. Oil does have its place in cake making but this is usually when fruit is to be added into the mix to add moisture. Vegetable oil does have a lower saturated fat content than butter (which is an animal fat).

If the cake is frozen, take it out of the freezer at least 4 hours before you start working on it to allow it to thaw slightly.

Always use eggs at room temperature. Add the beaten eggs slowly and beat thoroughly between additions. This gives the mixture a much paler colour, keeps the texture light and will ensure the mixture doesn't curdle. If it does, sift a tablespoon of flour into the mixture and fold it in with a figure of '8' motion using a metal spoon. The metal spoon will slice the mixture without pulling it and removing all the air you have already got into the cake mix. Once the flour is mixed in, continue to add the egg.

To test if the cake is baked, press the top with your fingers when you take it out of the oven. If it feels spongy and springs back it is ready. If you are still not sure, insert a skewer in the deepest part: it should draw back cleanly when the cake is cooked. Leave it in its tin until cold, then pack and store.

Before filling the cake, I always slice it in half and brush syrup over the two exposed sponge surfaces. I usually use vanilla but you can add other flavours such as toffee or cherry (see the recipe for cherry syrup in the black forest cake recipe, page 15). This is an excellent way of keeping the cake moist and accentuating the flavour.

Always use the best ingredients you can.

Cakes are always easier to carve if they have been frozen first, they are much less crumbly. If you prefer not to freeze the cake completely, wrap it in greaseproof paper then foil and secure with tape. Place in the fridge for at least 24 hours before carving.

Don't be tempted to keep opening the oven to look at the cake; leave it until around 10 minutes before the full time is up and have a quick look, not opening the oven fully. If the centre is still uncooked the cold air will make it sink. If you find that you are regularly getting sunken cakes, try adding a little more flour to the mix to make it a little stiffer, but bear in mind this can make the cake dryer.

how to line a cake tin

You can buy many specialist tins in various shapes, but I find they are not really necessary unless you are going to use them frequently. It is excellent value to buy the multi-size square tin with adjustable internal walls that can be positioned to make numerous rectangles and squares in different sizes (available from sugarcraft suppliers, see page 96). Mini cakes are now very popular so if you are making these you can buy mini cake pans in different shapes and sizes; these reduce the time involved in making mini cakes and ensure they all come out exactly the same size, something that would be very time consuming if you were cutting out the shapes by hand. Do bear in mind that once you make mini cakes, you also have to cover them individually so make sure you leave yourself enough time!

Before baking a cake the tin should always be lined with greaseproof paper to prevent the cake from sticking to the tin. The lining should be done neatly so that when the mixture is added it isn't distorted by the lining.

You will need:

Cake tin

Pencil

Greaseproof paper

Scissors

Butter

Pastry brush

1 Use a pencil to draw around the outside base of the tin on a sheet of greaseproof paper.

2 Cut out the shape a little inside the line to fit the base of the tin.

3 Cut a strip of greaseproof paper to fit around the sides of the tin with an overlap at the join. The strip should be approximately 2.5cm (1") deeper than the tin. It doesn't have to be in one whole piece but must overlap if in pieces.

4 Fold the strip along one long edge of the paper, approximately 1.3cm (½") from the edge. Unfold then snip along this side at regular intervals to make a fringe.

5 Melt some butter and, using a pastry brush, grease the side of the tin.

6 Insert the lining so the fringed edge lies on the base of the tin.

7 Grease the base of the tin and insert the base lining so it lies on top of the fringe, making a neat edge around the base of the tin.

8 Grease the lining with melted butter.

If you decide to use a spherical tin rather than carve the cake yourself, follow these instructions for lining the tin.

1 Cut out a circle of greaseproof paper that is 10cm (4") larger in diameter than the tin. Fold the circle in half twice to mark the centre point.

2 Cut from the outer edge towards the centre of the circle: stop approximately 2.5cm (1") from the centre so that you don't just cut the paper into pieces. Continue all the way round the circle to make segments that are joined together at the centre.

3 Grease the inside of the tin with melted butter. Place the centre of the liner in the centre of the tin then arrange the segments, overlapping them as you work around the tin. Use more melted butter to secure them in place.

4 Repeat to line the other half-sphere.

cake and icing recipes

Vanilla sponge							
Square	*12.5cm (5")*	*15cm (6")*	*17.5cm (7")*	*20.5cm (8")*	*23cm (9")*	*25.5cm (10")*	*28cm (11")*
Round	*15cm (6")*	*17.5cm (7")*	*20.5cm (8")*	*23cm (9")*	*25.5cm (10")*	*28cm (11")*	*30.5cm (12")*
Softened butter	175g (6oz)	260g (9oz)	430g (15oz)	510g (1lb 2oz)	690g (1lb 8oz)	770g (1lb 11oz)	940g (2lb 1oz)
Caster sugar	175g (6oz)	260g (9oz)	430g (15oz)	510g (1lb 2oz)	690g (1lb 8oz)	770g (1lb 11oz)	940g (2lb 1oz)
Eggs (medium)	3	4	7	8	10	11	13
Self-raising flour	225g (8oz)	340g (12oz)	560g (1lb 4oz)	700g (1lb 8oz)	1kg (2lb 3oz)	1.14kg (2lb 8oz)	1.3kg (2lb 14oz)
Vanilla essence	½tsp	1tsp	2½tsp	3tsp	4tsp	4½tsp	5½tsp
Baking times	¾–1 hour	1–1 hour 10 minutes	1¼–1 hour 20 minutes	1½–1 hour 40 minutes	1¾–2 hours	2¼–2½ hours	2½–2¾ hours

1 Beat the butter and sugar together until fluffy and light in colour.

2 Beat the eggs, then add them to the mixture a little at a time, beating in thoroughly before adding more. If the mixture looks like it is splitting, add in a tablespoon of the flour.

3 Fold in the flour using a metal spoon.

4 Add the vanilla essence.

5 Transfer the mixture to the prepared baking tin, making sure that it is slightly lower in the centre.

6 Bake in a preheated oven at 180°C/350°F/gas mark 4, until the cake is a golden brown colour and springy to the touch.

Variation: lemon cake

- Substitute the vanilla in the recipe for concentrated lemon juice.

- When making the buttercream, add 10–20ml (½–¾fl oz) of lemon juice.

Variation: simple chocolate cake

- Add 25g (1oz) of cocoa for every 225g (8oz) of flour and 15ml (1tbsp) of milk for each 25g (1oz) of cocoa to ensure that the mixture is not too dry.

Chocolate sponge								
Square	12.5cm (5")	15cm (6")	17.5cm (7")	20.5cm (8")	23cm (9")	25.5cm (10")	28cm (11")	30.5cm (12")
Round	15cm (6")	17.5cm (7")	20.5cm (8")	23cm (9")	25.5cm (10")	28cm (11")	30.5cm (12")	33cm (13")
Softened butter	85g (2¾oz)	115g (4oz)	150g (5¼oz)	225g (8oz)	310g (10¾oz)	340g (12oz)	425g (14¾oz)	510g (1lb 2oz)
Soft brown sugar	195g (6¾oz)	285g (10oz)	450g (1lb)	560g (1lb 4oz)	720g (1lb 10oz)	860g (1lb 14oz)	1kg (2lb 3oz)	1.25kg (2lb 12oz)
Cocoa powder	20g (¾oz)	30g (1oz)	50g (1¾oz)	60g (2oz)	80g (2¾oz)	90g (3oz)	110g (3¾oz)	120g (4¼oz)
Water	60ml (2fl oz)	90ml (3fl oz)	145ml (5fl oz)	175ml (6fl oz)	225ml (8fl oz)	260ml (9fl oz)	315ml (11fl oz)	370ml (13fl oz)
Plain flour	150g (5¼oz)	225g (8oz)	375g (13¼oz)	450g (1lb)	750g (1lb 10oz)	800g (1lb 12oz)	1.1kg (2lb 6oz)	1.35kg (3lb)
Baking powder	1¼tsp	2tsp	2½tsp	4tsp	4tsp	6tsp	7¼tsp	8½tsp
Bicarbonate of soda + salt	⅓tsp	½tsp	1¼tsp	2tsp	3tsp	3¾tsp	4tsp	4¼tsp
Vanilla essence	1tsp	1tsp	1¼tsp	2tsp	3tsp	3¾tsp	4tsp	4¼tsp
Eggs (large)	2	2	3	4	5	6	7	8
Sour cream	75ml (2½fl oz)	150ml (5fl oz)	200ml (7fl oz)	300ml (10½fl oz)	335ml (11¾fl oz)	450ml (15½fl oz)	540ml (19½fl oz)	580ml (1pt)
Baking times	¾–1 hour	1–1 hour 10 minutes	1¼–1 hour 20 minutes	1½–1 hours 40 minutes	1¾–2 hours	2¼–2½ hours	2½–2¾ hours	2¾–3 hours

1 Sift all the dry ingredients into a bowl.

2 Beat the butter and sugar together until light and fluffy in texture.

3 Beat the eggs and add to the butter mixture a little at a time. If the mixture looks like it is going to split, add a tablespoon of the dry ingredients, then continue adding the egg.

4 Add the vanilla essence and beat well. Add the sour cream and mix gently.

5 Fold the dry ingredients into the mixture using a metal spoon. Only add the water if the mixture is too stiff.

6 Carefully spoon the mixture into the prepared cake tin and bake in the centre of the oven for the suggested time at 190°C/370°F/gas mark 5.

Variation: chocolate and cherry cake

- Add 90g (3oz) of dried or glacé cherries to the basic recipe.

Variation: black forest chocolate cake

- Add 45ml (3tbsp) of cherry brandy to the cake for every 225g (8oz) of flour. For a non-alcoholic version, use 225g (8oz) of morello cherries with 225g (8oz) of sugar and 100ml (3½fl oz) of water. Boil the ingredients together until the cherries are soft, mash with a potato masher and sieve to remove the skins and other fleshy bits.

- Add 400g (14oz) of tinned cherries in syrup for every 250g (8¾oz) of flour. Roughly chop the cherries and save the syrup or make the syrup as above if using fresh cherries.

- Add the cherry syrup to the buttercream filling.

alcoholic cake recipes

We are all used to using alcohol in fruit cakes, feeding them regularly with brandy to give a deliciously moist cake for the celebration. But what about alcohol in sponge cakes? Alcohol can be used to give a distinct flavour to your baking, perfect if you are making a cake for a man's birthday or Father's Day. Be adventurous and try flavours used in cocktails: if they work in a glass, chances are they will work in a cake! If you would rather not bake with alcohol, you can always add it to the buttercream filling.

Remember to let your guests know that the cake does contain alcohol; leave it out completely if any children will be at the celebration.

Black Russian sponge cake

This delicious cake has a chocolate sponge base with *crème de cacao* and Kahlúa.

To give an authentic Black Russian flavour, add 15ml (1tbsp) vodka, 15ml (1tbsp) Kahlúa and 10ml (²/₃tbsp) *crème de cacao* to the 15cm (6") round chocolate cake mix recipe. Adjust the volume if making more or less mixture, or adjust to taste.

To fill the cake, make the buttercream in the usual way (see page 17) but add 45g (1½oz) extra icing sugar with 15ml (1tbsp) vodka, 15ml (1tbsp) Kahlúa 15ml (1tbsp) *crème de cacao* and 15ml (1tbsp) cocoa powder to the mixture. Taste and adjust as required. Remember of course this isn't going to be baked so will be as potent as its constituent parts.

Piña colada sponge cake

This is the perfect flavour for a summer cake – the fresh pineapple and coconut with a rum kick will make you feel warm and tropical!

Chop 4 thin slices of fresh pineapple into tiny chunks, place in a bowl and pour 55ml (3tbsp) of white rum over the top. Leave to soak for a couple of hours. Add this and 55ml (3tbsp) of coconut milk to the 15cm (6") round vanilla sponge cake mix and bake in the usual way. Adjust the volume if making more or less mixture.

To flavour the cake filling, make the buttercream in the usual way but add 45g (1½oz) extra icing sugar with 2 slices of chopped pineapple that has been soaked in 15ml (1tbsp) white rum and 35ml (2tbsp) coconut milk.

Apricot brandy sponge cake

This is just an example of how to use a fruit flavoured liqueur, of which there are many! Chop up 15 dried apricots into small pieces, then soak the fruit in 45–60ml (3–4tbsp) of apricot brandy for a couple of hours. Add this to the vanilla sponge cake mixture. This is sufficient for a 15cm (6") round cake mix, so increase or decrease the volume according to the size of your cake.

Buttercream

The quantity of buttercream required is given at the beginning of each project so scale the ingredients up or down as needed. This recipe makes approximately 1.2kg (2lb 11oz) of icing, or enough to fill and cover a 28cm (11") round cake.

You will need:

225g (8oz) butter, softened

1kg (2lb 3¼oz) icing sugar

15–30ml (1–2tbsp) syrup (vanilla or a flavour of your choice to complement the cake) or fresh fruit juice

1 Beat the butter and add the icing sugar in small amounts until it is all incorporated and the mixture is smooth.

2 Add the syrup/flavouring a little at a time until the buttercream has a soft consistency; add more if a softer texture is needed (you might find this when crumb-coating the surface of cakes as a softer icing won't pull the cake into crumbs).

Sugar syrup

I use this for sprinkling over the cut slices of cake to add extra moisture and flavour.

You will need:

250ml (8¾fl oz) water

250g (8¾oz) caster sugar

1 Combine both ingredients in a saucepan, heat to dissolve the sugar and bring to the boil. Continue boiling until the volume has reduced by a quarter.

2 Allow to cool before use. The syrup can be stored in a sterilised jar in the fridge for up to 1 month.

Royal icing

You will need:

2 egg whites from British Lion-marked eggs (or SK Fortified Albumen if you prefer not to use fresh eggs)

455g (1lb) icing sugar, sieved

1 Place the egg whites in a bowl and sieve the icing sugar over the top. Mix in thoroughly.

2 Keep adding icing sugar until the required consistency is achieved. For most applications in this book, the icing needs to be a little stiffer than runny; if it is too stiff, it will not act as a 'glue' to stick decorations in place.

To save time you can buy Instant Mix Royal Icing from Squires Kitchen (see page 96).

Ganache

If you would like to fill the chocolate cake with a deliciously rich chocolate filling, ganache is the perfect choice! Follow the buttercream quantities given at the beginning of the projects as a guide; this recipe is enough to fill and cover a 23cm (9") cake. To save time you can buy it readymade from Squires Kitchen (see suppliers on page 96).

You will need:

500g (1lb 1½oz) dark chocolate, chopped

250ml (8¾fl oz) double cream

125g (4½oz) unsalted butter

1 Place the chopped, dark chocolate into a heatproof bowl.

2 Heat the cream and butter in a high-sided saucepan until it just starts to boil. Pour this over the chocolate and stir until smooth.

3 Leave the ganache to cool and harden then store in the fridge until required. If it is too stiff to spread, gently warm it in a double boiler (*bain marie*) to bring it to spreading consistency.

recipes using cake crumbs

Once you have carved a cake there can be a few cake crumbs left over. Rather than waste them, you can incorporate them into other recipes such as these scrumptious cookies.

If you don't have time to do anything with the cake crumbs when they're fresh, seal in small quantities in plastic food bags and freeze until you have more time. You should only do this if the cake has not already been frozen and thawed (see page 12).

Cake crumb cookies

You will need:

150g (5¼oz) butter

150g (5¼oz) granulated sugar

150g (5¼oz) golden syrup (I use maple flavour – delicious!)

150g (5¼oz) self-raising flour

250g (8¾oz) cake crumbs

1 Preheat the oven to 200°C/400°F/gas mark 6. Crumble the cake into crumbs and spread into one layer on a baking tray. Place at the top of a hot oven for 5 minutes or until a light toasted brown colour. Remove the crumbs and leave the oven on.

TIP

The crumbs need to be toasted otherwise the biscuits are not as crunchy.

2 Melt the butter, sugar and golden syrup in a pan. Leave to cool slightly.

3 Add the flour to the melted ingredients and mix well.

4 Add the cake crumbs and mix well.

5 Take heaped teaspoonfuls of the mixture, roll into balls, place on a baking sheet and flatten slightly. Bake in an oven for 6–9 minutes until golden.

Truffles

You will need:

125g (4½oz) dark chocolate

50g (1¾oz) unsalted butter

125g (4½oz) cake crumbs

50g (1¾oz) icing sugar

25ml (1tbsp) dark rum, brandy, or liqueur of your choice, or chocolate syrup for a non-alcoholic version

Chopped nuts, chocolate vermicelli, or cocoa powder (for coating)

1 Melt the chocolate and butter in a non-stick pan or in a microwave.

2 Add the cake crumbs, icing sugar and liqueur and mix well.

3 Place in the fridge for half an hour or so until the mixture starts to firm up.

4 Take about a teaspoon of mixture, shape into a ball and roll in the coating of your choice.

5 Leave to cool thoroughly in the fridge.

TIP

These work really well as gifts – place in little petits fours cases and present in a gift box. Alternatively, make cake pops by inserting a lolly stick and dipping into melted chocolate. Decorate with vermicelli or sugar sprinkles.

Refrigerator cake

You will need:

350g (12¼oz) dark chocolate

125g (4½oz) butter

35ml (2tbsp) golden syrup

450g (1lb) cake crumbs (whizz them in a food processor if the crumbs are not fine enough)

75ml (4tbsp) rum (or amaretto if you are using amaretto biscuits) or chocolate syrup for a non-alcoholic version

225g (8oz) crushed digestive biscuits (or amaretto biscuits)

50g (1¾oz) glacé cherries, roughly chopped

50g (1¾oz) sultanas (optional)

20.5cm (8") square cake tin, lined with greaseproof paper (bring the paper over the sides of the tin to make it easier to lift out the cake when set)

1 If you are using sultanas in the recipe, soak them in the rum/amaretto/chocolate syrup for 1 hour before making the cake.

2 Melt the chocolate, butter and golden syrup in a non-stick pan or in a microwave.

3 Add the cake crumbs and crushed biscuits. Stir thoroughly.

4 Add the glacé cherries and soaked sultanas if you are using them; if not, add the rum/amaretto/syrup at this stage too. Mix well.

5 Pour into the prepared tin and refrigerate for 1–2 hours until set.

6 Slice into 18 finger-sized slices.

Bakewell tart topping

You will need:

50g (1¾oz) butter (softened)

50g (1¾oz) sugar

1 egg

50g (1¾oz) ground almonds

Almond essence

50g (1¾oz) cake crumbs

1 Beat the sugar and butter together until they are light and fluffy.

2 Add the egg and beat.

3 Add the ground almonds, almond essence and cake crumbs and mix well.

This makes a delicious topping for a Bakewell tart, giving it a more substantial texture than the traditional sponge topping.

TIP

You can always use up your cake crumbs in any recipe that asks for a biscuit base such as cheesecake or tart au chocolat – simply replace the biscuits in the recipe with cake crumbs.

portion chart

It is not always easy to work out how many portions you will get from a carved cake as they have been altered from their original shape, so I have included an approximate number of servings with each project. Remember that this will vary depending on how you slice the cake. If you need to increase the amount of cake for your guests, this chart gives an estimate for the number of slices you will get from each cake size, cutting the cake into rectangular shapes rather than wedges. Bear in mind that this is only a guideline: if you're unsure whether you will have enough cake, you can make it larger (remember to increase the amount of sugarpaste and buttercream too, see page 25) or bake cupcakes to match the main cake.

Size	Round	Square
12.5cm (5")	7	8
15cm (6")	11	14
17.5cm (7")	15	20
20.5cm (8")	20	27
23cm (9")	27	35
25.5cm (10")	34	45
28cm (11")	43	56
30.5cm (12")	50	67

guide to using templates

All of the templates required for the projects in this book are supplied at the back (see pages 93 to 95). There are instructions for enlarging them to the correct size, although you can make the cake bigger or smaller to suit the number of guests.

You will need:

Greaseproof/tracing paper

Pencil

Thin card or an empty cereal packet

Sharp scissors or a craft knife and cutting board

Glass-headed pins, sterilized

Small, sharp knife

1 Enlarge the template to the size required using a photocopier or scanner.

2 Trace the shape onto greaseproof or tracing paper and cut out. If you are making a basic shape, use this as your template. For more elaborate shapes, trace the shape onto thin card and cut out.

3 Pin the template to the cake using glass-headed pins that have been sterilized with alcohol or boiling water.

4 Following the template, carefully carve the cake using a small, sharp knife.

TIP

Always use glass-headed pins because they are easier to see. Count the pins out as you use them and make sure you put them all away safely afterwards.

5 Remove the template and put the pins away safely. Use the knife to round off the edges of the cake.

6 Continue to create the shape required, following the step photographs as a guide.

preparing a cake

Trimming

For the most part, carved novelty cakes do not need to be trimmed (the brown crust removed from the outside of the cake) because as you cut your novelty cake to shape, you will most likely remove this anyway. If you have any left showing when you have finished, you can decide if it needs to be removed. As long as the crust isn't burnt I don't usually trim it off as it tastes as delicious as the rest of the cake.

Levelling

No matter how carefully you level the cake mixture before cooking, you will almost certainly find that it will rise and leave a domed top when baked. If the top isn't too raised or crispy you could leave it, turn it upside down so you have the flat base as the top of the cake and fill the gap around the bottom of the cake with small sausages of sugarpaste. This is particularly useful if your cake is rather shallow in depth as trimming the top flat would make it even shallower. Try to aim for around 7.5cm (3") as a depth for your cakes. If you find that they are consistently shallow in the tin despite following the correct amount of mix, make more mix to ensure that the tin is approximately ¾ full before baking. (Recommended quantities are given on pages 14 to 15.)

You will need:

Side marker (Kit Box)

Ruler

Long, serrated knife

Palette knife

Spare cake drum or board

Small spirit level

 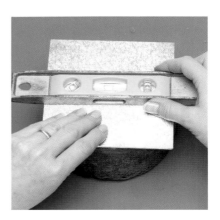

1 To trim the top of a cake to a constant depth, use a side marker. Measure the lowest depth of the cake with the ruler, set the side marker to this depth, then scribe a line all the way round the top of cake as a cutting guide.

2 Follow the scribed line with the long, serrated knife, cutting carefully towards the centre of the cake. If you work your way around the cake, not going too deeply, you will find it easier to keep the cutting level. Remove the top crust and turn the cake over so you now have the bottom of the cake at the top.

3 Place a spare cake drum or board on top of the cake with the spirit level on top. Check that the cake is completely level.

Cutting and filling

1 Measure the cake again and set the side marker to scribe a line all the way round the centre of the cake. If the cake is deep, set the marker at 2–3cm (approximately 1") intervals.

2 Using the long, serrated knife, cut into the centre of the cake along the scribed line as before.

3 Remove the top layer of cake by sliding it onto a spare cake drum. This is the easiest way to remove the cake without it breaking into pieces.

4 Fill the cake with buttercream using the palette knife, then replace the top section of cake by sliding it carefully from the drum back onto the cake.

covering a cake

Following these steps to cover your cakes will ensure that your cake has a professional appearance and gives you the perfect surface on which to complete your design.

You will need:

Cake and filling

Large, serrated knife

Spare cake drum

Palette knife or spatula

Sugarpaste (see each project for the quantity required)

Paste food colours (SK)

Large rolling pin

2 cake smoothers

Small, cranked palette knife

Spacers

Cocktail stick

Icing sugar in shaker

1 Prepare the cake by trimming, levelling, cutting and filling with your chosen flavour of buttercream (see pages 21 to 22). If the cake is deep (such as the safari vehicle), slice the cake every 2–3cm (approximately 1") so there is plenty of filling through the cake. Cut to shape following the instructions for your chosen project.

2 Using a palette knife or spatula, cover the outside of the sponge cake with a thin layer of buttercream: this will help the sugarpaste stick to the cake and will keep any crumbs stuck to the cake and not in the sugarpaste. This is known as the crumb coating. Always prepare

the cake to this stage before rolling out the sugarpaste, otherwise the paste will start to dry and crack when covering the cake.

3 Colour the sugarpaste with paste colouring if required and roll out on a surface dusted lightly with icing sugar. Roll out using a large rolling pin, using spacers if you wish to ensure the paste is the same thickness throughout.

4 Check that the paste is the correct size by roughly measuring the top and sides of the cake with the rolling pin. The paste should be approximately 3–4mm ($^1/_8$") thick. Gently roll the paste over the rolling pin and transfer it to the cake. Carefully unroll the sugarpaste over the cake, making sure there is enough hanging over the cake sides to cover the cake completely.

5 Smooth the top of the cake gently with the palms of your hands, making sure there are no pockets of trapped air under the surface. Continue smoothing gently over the edge, allowing the paste to adhere to the cake, and continue smoothing the paste carefully down the sides of the cake.

6 Allow the excess paste to flatten out onto the cake drum and then use a sharp knife to trim it off, leaving about 5mm (just over $^1/_8$") still flat on the board.

7 Smooth the sides of the cake further and flatten the excess paste on the cake drum. Trim all the excess off to make a neat edge around the base.

8 Using two smoothers with the sharp corner edges at the bottom, smooth the sides of the cake evenly, paying particular

attention to the trimmed edge of the paste. Gently smooth the top of the cake with the smoothers.

TIP

For rounded cakes, you may wish to skip this step as the smoothers have a flat surface.

9 Make a pad of the same colour sugarpaste and flatten on the work surface to make sure the pad is smooth and free from cracks and lumps. Lightly 'polish' the cake with the pad, removing any grains of icing sugar and leaving a shiny, smooth surface. Pay particular attention to the curve of the paste over the top edge to smooth out any fine cracks in the paste.

 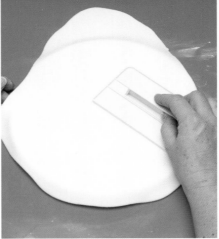 

covering a cake drum

Cake drums are 15mm thick, foil-covered cake boards that are used under the base of cakes. They come in all sorts of shapes and sizes, including round, square, oval and petal. All of the cakes in this book are presented on cake drums covered with sugarpaste and trimmed with co-ordinating ribbon.

You will need:

Cake drum (see each project for the shape and size required)

Kitchen roll

Cooled, boiled water

Sugarpaste

Icing sugar shaker

Large rolling pin

Sugarpaste

Smoother

Spacers (optional)

Sharp knife

Pizza wheel

Small turntable (optional)

15mm width ribbon, long enough to cover the edge of the cake drum

Non-toxic glue stick or double-sided tape

1 Lightly dampen the cake drum using kitchen roll dampened with cooled, boiled water, just enough to allow the sugarpaste to stick.

2 Lightly dust the work surface with icing sugar, then roll out the paste using a large rolling pin. You can use spacers to keep the thickness of paste even.

3 Roll out the paste into the general shape of the cake drum to be covered, until it is slightly larger than the cake drum. It should be approximately 5mm (¹/₈") thick.

4 Lift the paste onto the cake drum, using the rolling pin to help move the paste without stretching or tearing it.

5 Using the cake smoother, smooth the paste on the cake drum.

6 Cut around the edge of the drum with a sharp knife to remove the excess paste. Hold the knife against the edge of the drum as you cut to keep the edge straight.

7 Form a pad with the paste trimmings and smooth the cut edge, taking care not to tear it.

8 Apply some non-toxic glue to the edge of the drum, taking care not to come into contact with the sugarpaste covering. Alternatively, attach small pieces of double-sided tape around the edge of the drum. Carefully attach a length of ribbon around the edge, overlapping the join at the back by approximately 2.5cm (1").

cake covering quantities

All the cake sizes for the projects in this book are given at the beginning, but if you would like to make them bigger or smaller to suit the number of recipients, you can use this chart as a guide to the amount of cake filling and covering that you will need.

Cake size	Buttercream/ganache	Sugarpaste covering	Sugarpaste for drum
10cm (4")	150g (5¼oz)	500g (1lb 1½oz)	100g (3½oz)
12.5cm (5")	225g (8oz)	600g (1lb 5¼oz)	150g (5¼oz)
15cm (6")	300g (10½oz)	700g (1lb 8¾oz)	200g (7¼oz)
18cm (7")	450g (1lb)	750g (1lb 10½oz)	250g (8¾oz)
20.5cm (8")	600g (1lb 5¼oz)	1.25kg (2lb 12¼oz)	300g (10½oz)
23cm (9")	750g (1lb 10½oz)	1.5kg (3lb 5oz)	325g (11½oz)
25.5cm (10")	1kg (2lb 3¼oz)	2kg (4lb 6½oz)	400g (14¼oz)
28cm (11")	1.25kg (2lb 12¼oz)	2.2kg (4lb 13½oz)	475g (1lb ¾oz)
30.5cm (12")	1.5kg (3lb 5oz)	2.4kg (5lb 4½oz)	500g (1lb 1½oz)
33cm (13")	1.75kg (3lb 13¾oz)	2.75kg (6lb 1oz)	550g (1lb 3½oz)
35.5cm (14")	2kg (4lb 6½oz)	3kg (6lb 9¾oz)	575g (1lb 4¼oz)

rugby scrum

Edibles

23cm (9") square cake

300g (10½oz) buttercream

3kg (6lb 9¾oz) sugarpaste: black

SK Mexican Modelling Paste (MMP): 600g
(1lb 5¼oz) Black, 1kg (2lb 3¼oz) White

50g (1¾oz) SK Instant Mix Royal Icing

SK Paste Food Colours: Chestnut, Jet
Black, Marigold

SK Piping Gel

White vegetable fat

Equipment

Basic equipment (see pages 6 to 9)

25.5cm (10") oval cake drum

Slices: approximately 35

I had never studied rugby scrums in such detail before I made this cake! Any rugby player who has been in the
middle of a scrum is sure to appreciate the mass of bodies and the mix of arms and legs!

1 Place the cake with the flat base uppermost on the work surface. Mark out an oval on the base of the cake, then start cutting the shape out using a sharp knife.

2 To shape the cake into a rough oval, use the sharp knife to take off the top edges of the cake and continue shaping the top of the cake at an angle.

3 Continue forming the cake into an oval dome shape by slicing off small pieces at a time.

4 Use the mini palette knife to trim the cake further, taking finer slices of cake away from the top, sides and base to round off the surface. Stop and look at the shape every few minutes, working around the cake slowly and carefully.

5 Cover the cake drum with 700g (1lb 8¾oz) of black sugarpaste. Smooth with a pad of paste to remove any traces of icing sugar then leave to dry.

6 Cut the cake in half and fill with buttercream and/or jam (see pages 21 to 22), then cover the outside of the cake with buttercream.

7 Roll out the remaining black sugarpaste and cover the cake. Smooth the paste over the surface of the oval and trim around the base. Smooth with a pad of paste to remove any traces of icing sugar then position the cake in the centre of the cake drum.

8 The rugby scrum is put together with several figures all made the same way but with odd body parts missing, depending on their position in the scrum: the props and hookers in the centre don't have heads or legs as they are tucked down and linked with their opponents; the next row have only the backs of their heads

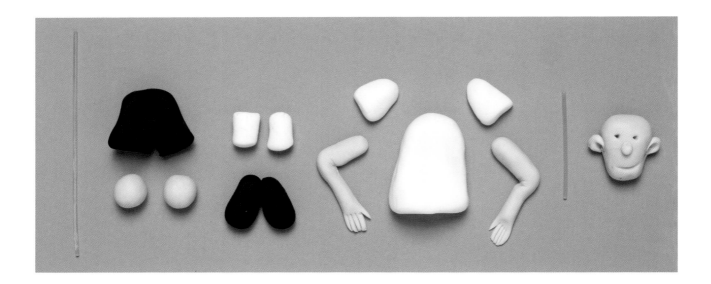

and don't have the lower part of their legs; and only the outside players have all their limbs. Follow the step picture to make the various shapes, starting with a row of bodies then adding the arms and short sleeves. Look at where the arms are positioned so they look as natural as possible.

9 The legs are made up of knees and white socks that are stuck together with the shorts at the top and shoes at the bottom. Use edible glue to stick each piece together and use strands of spaghetti as extra support if required. Use the flower shaping tool to mark creases on the clothing to make them more realistic.

10 Colour 30g (1oz) of the royal icing with Jet Black paste colour, place it into a piping bag with a no. 1 nozzle and pipe the numbers on the shirts. (I have piped random numbers on the players but you may wish to be more technically correct with the position of the players, or even pipe the age of the recipient on each one.)

11 Colour the remaining royal icing with a little Chestnut paste colour and dab it all over the cake board and on some of the players with a paintbrush to give a muddy appearance. When dry, add a little piping gel over the top to give a wet look.

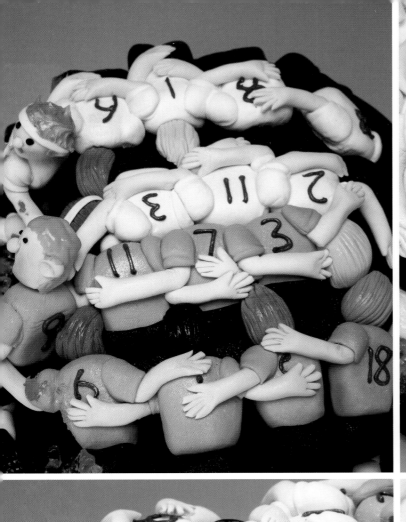

alien

Edibles

3 x 10cm (4")* and 3 x 20.5cm (8") round cakes

300g (10½oz) buttercream

3kg (6lb 9¾oz) sugarpaste: white

SK Mexican Modelling Paste (MMP): 50g (1¾oz) Black, 600g (1lb 5¼oz) White

SK Paste Food Colours: Holly/Ivy, Leaf Green, Nasturtium, Rose, Violet

SK Metallic Lustre Dust Food Colour: Snowflake

White vegetable fat

* Use the same quantity of cake mix as for a 17.5cm (7") round cake (see pages 14 to 15).

Equipment

Basic equipment (see pages 6 to 9)

6 cake dowels

25.5cm (10") round cake drum

Pack of 22-gauge floral wires: white

Bubbles texture mat (SA)

3 posy picks

Slices:
approximately 48

This three-eyed alien is a great cake for little boys with a big imagination!

1 Level and fill the three 20.5cm (8") cakes then stack them on top of each other in one large block.

2 Using a ruler and sharp knife, cut two dowelling rods to 20.5cm (8"). Push one of the dowels down through the centre of the cakes from the top: this gives you a height guide when trimming the cake. Lay the other dowel horizontally across the top for a width guide.

3 Start trimming the cake stack into a ball shape: cut the top edge off in sections first with a large knife to get the general shape, then use a small knife to gradually create the ball shape. Turn the cake frequently to ensure the shape is even. When you have finished, take the dowelling rod out of the cake.

4 Repeat the above steps with the smaller cakes to make the second ball. The larger ball will form the body and the smaller will be the head.

5 Colour 500g (1lb 1½oz) of white sugarpaste with Leaf Green paste colour. Cover the small ball (i.e. the head) with this paste then trim and smooth the ball for a neat finish. Keep the excess paste sealed in a polythene bag for later.

6 Prepare the body of the alien by adding a pad of paste to the front of the ball to increase the girth. Use buttercream to stick it in place.

7 Colour 1.5kg (3lb 5oz) of white sugarpaste with a little Rose paste colour to achieve a light pink colour. Cover the ball with buttercream then roll out the paste and cover the ball. Smooth with a pad of paste, cut away the excess at the base and use the flower shaping tool to texture the front of the belly with deep lines, marking them closer together as you work upwards.

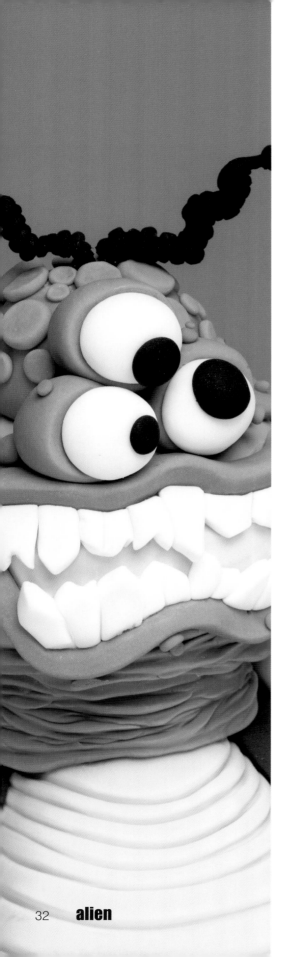

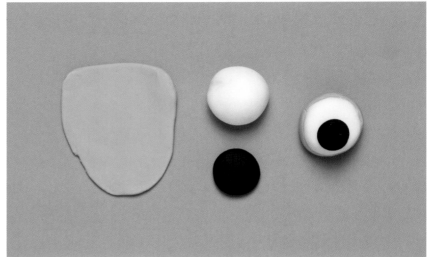

8 Cover the cake drum with 500g (1lb 1½oz) of sugarpaste that has been very lightly coloured with Vine paste colour. Whilst the paste is still soft, texture the surface with the bubble texture mat. Leave to dry.

9 Position the body onto the cake drum towards the back.

10 Make the purple skin of the alien from 500g (1lb 1½oz) of sugarpaste coloured with Violet paste colour. Cut this paste in half and work each piece into an egg shape. Flatten the broad base with a rolling pin and lengthen slightly. Attach to each side of the alien body with edible glue, allowing it to wrap around the back of the alien body. Cut and trim into place. Roll the remnants of paste into a rectangle to completely cover the back of the body.

11 Push two full-length cake dowels down through the neck and into the body and push the head over them. Sandwich the two cakes together with buttercream.

12 Colour 300g (10½oz) of White MMP with Holly/Ivy paste colour. Roll 100g (3½oz) of this paste into a sausage and wrap it around the neck, securing in place with edible glue. Use the flower shaping tool to create all the creases in the neck.

13 Shape the lips of the alien from 50g (1¾oz) of the Holly/Ivy paste and secure them in place with edible glue.

14 Colour 150g (5¼oz) of White MMP orange using the Nasturtium paste colour. Use 75g (2½oz) to make a flattened ball for the top of the head and secure in place with edible glue.

15 Shape two feet from 50g (1¾oz) of the orange paste by making two flattened balls. Cut off a third to make a flattened end, then take a 'v' shaped wedge out. Shape four claws from 10g (¼oz) of Violet paste and attach to the feet. Position up against the body on the cake drum and secure with edible glue.

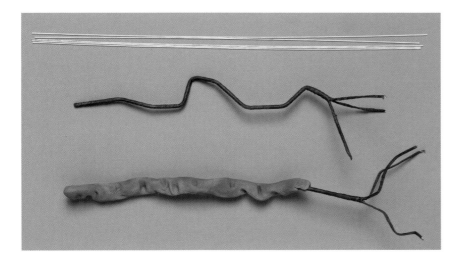

16 Roll the remaining orange paste into various shaped balls and attach these to the head of the alien using edible glue.

17 Make three white balls from MMP for the eyes, then cover the back of the balls with rolled out green MMP reserved from earlier. Add a pupil to each eye and secure the eyes above the mouth using edible glue.

18 Use the remnants of green paste to make flattened green balls on the Violet parts of the alien.

19 Roll out some White MMP and use a craft knife to cut out rough rectangles with jagged tops for the teeth. Attach to the mouth using edible glue, pushing them together as you work.

20 Make the arms of the alien using several 22-gauge wires. Tape the wires together using black floral tape, then attach shorter wires to make fingers. Bend the wires at different angles.

21 Colour 100g (3½oz) of MMP with Violet paste colour. Roll into a rough sausage shape and attach it to the wire using edible glue. Roughly squeeze the paste onto the wire to give a bumpy effect.

22 Attach each arm to the body by inserting the wires into a posy pick filled with paste, then push this into the top of the body, just below the neck. Secure a green ball around the entry point using edible glue.

23 To make the antennae, roll some Black MMP into a thin sausage and wrap it around a single 22-gauge wire, twisting and coiling it as you go. Make another antenna in the same way, then insert the wires into a single posy pick filled with paste and push the pick into the top of the head. Add two balls to the ends of the wires using edible glue.

microcar

Edibles

20.5cm (8") square cake

3kg (6lb 9¾oz) sugarpaste: white

300g (10½oz) SK Mexican Modelling
Paste (MMP): Black

225g (8oz) buttercream

SK Paste Food Colours: Daffodil, Fern,
Poppy

SK Edible Metallic Paint: Silver

SK Edible Glue

Equipment

Basic equipment (see pages 6 to 9)

23cm (9") round cake drum

SK Great Impressions Wheel Mould: large

Car template (see page 93)

Slices: approximately 28

The following instructions will allow you to make any model of car you wish – they are all made the same way
by sourcing photographs, drawings or blueprints of your chosen car. As long as the material shows all aspects
of the car, you can get accurate measurements at every angle, so you can ensure that any car you carve will be
accurate in dimension, a huge step forward in recreating your favourite car in cake. Should you want a car larger
or smaller than the source material you have found, simply enlarge or reduce it on a photocopier or on the
computer. Make sure you get some pictures of the car in colour so you can colour the sugarpaste to match.

1 Colour 500g (1lb 1½oz) of white sugarpaste with Fern paste colour, roll out and cover the cake drum. Save the remnants of paste for later to make the tufts of grass.

2 Trace a template of the outline of the car, then add a few basic elements to the template to mark the important features on the car. Use a sharp knife to cut out the car shape from the cake. Make sure that you don't undercut the cake at the base as this will make one side of your car smaller than the other.

3 Using the mini palette knife, trim the edges off the car to soften the overall shape. However, if this is not a feature of your chosen car, leave the edges sharp.

TIP

Modern cars tend to be sleek with smooth lines but older or vintage cars are more boxy, so follow the pattern of your car.

4 Shape the wheel arches with the mini palette knife, carving in by just a few millimetres. Repeat on both sides.

5 Cut away the sections where the wheels will go on both sides but don't cut in too far otherwise the car will not be stable. Make sure the cake stands upright on both sets of wheels.

6 Use the mini palette knife to carve outlines into the cake, not too deeply but enough to give you the position for the various features of the car.

7 Mark the edges of the windscreen and cut away slightly to leave a slight indentation.

8 Cover the cake with a thin layer of buttercream. Thinly roll out 500g (1lb 1½oz) of white sugarpaste and cover the cake to give a smooth base and keep crumbs away from the finished covering. Place onto the covered cake drum.

9 Use small sausages of white sugarpaste to pad out the wheel arches on the car. (This is a feature of the car I chose but may not be necessary for your car.) Use edible glue to secure them in place and smooth them well onto the cake so there are no unsightly lines on the finished covering.

10 Roll out 100g (3½oz) of Black MMP into a long, thin strip and use the ribbon cutter to cut a strip 2.5cm (1") wide. Attach this all the way around the base of the car with edible glue, including into the wheel arches.

11 Starting at the back of the car, use the pointed end of the flower shaping tool to map out the sections of the car. This will enable you to keep the features of the car in proportion.

12 Colour 1kg (2lb 3¼oz) of white sugarpaste with Daffodil paste colour. This will give you enough to cover the whole car, so keep any unused paste sealed in a plastic bag whilst you are working.

TIP

Colouring all the paste for the cake covering in one go means that you have a uniform colour to use throughout the project – you don't want the bonnet to be a different colour to the boot!

13 Roll out some of the Daffodil-coloured paste to a thickness of 5mm (¹/₈") and cover the back of the car up to the marking for the black roof section. Cut with a sharp craft knife to ensure the edges are neat. Tuck the paste into the wheel arches and under the bumper and trim off the excess.

14 Fill the black roof section next using 50g (1¾oz) of Black MMP. Cut a straight

line using the craft knife or pizza wheel then attach this edge to the top of the boot section to give a sharp finish. Trim the side and top of the roof using the craft knife following the lines you drew on the cake.

15 Use the remnants cut from the roof to form the spoiler for the back. Shape into an elongated triangle and attach to the car with edible glue.

16 Cover the roof next using 50g (1¾oz) of white sugarpaste. Roll out into a rough square the same thickness as the black roof section. Cut a straight line using the pizza wheel and apply this up against the black roof section. Trim the sides and front using a craft knife. Cut a smooth curve in preparation for the window. Apply edible glue under this section once you are happy with the shape and secure it in place.

17 Continue along the side of the car. Complete the next part which is a continuation of the main roof. This section is best cut from a template, so take a template to fit your cake using greaseproof

paper by holding a sheet lightly against the car and tracing the shape onto the paper using a pencil. Cut this piece from 25g (1oz) of white sugarpaste, hold it against the car to check the shape, then attach using edible glue. Repeat on the other side.

18 Use the same technique as step 17 to make the car doors from 50g (1¾oz) of the Daffodil sugarpaste. Smooth the piece into place and secure with edible glue.

19 Cover the black handle at the back of the car doors using two small pinches of Black MMP shaped into triangles. Secure in place on both sides.

20 Make a rough template for the side windows using greaseproof paper and pencil as before. Roll out approximately 25g (1oz) of white sugarpaste fairly thinly and cut out the template shape neatly with a craft knife. Position a window on each door and secure in place with edible glue.

21 Next, insert the black roof strut that runs around the front of the side

window. Use a pinch of Black MMP for this and make sure it is slightly deeper than the window to keep the side window recessed.

22 To cover the car wings and bonnet you will need 100g (3½oz) of the Daffodil paste. Roll out the paste and lay it smoothly onto the bonnet, curving the paste around the wings and pushing it neatly up against the car doors. Trim around the windscreen using a craft knife to achieve a sharp finish. Smooth the paste over the wings, into the wheel arches and under the bumper section. Cut off any excess paste with the craft knife.

23 Fill in the front windscreen with approximately 25g (1oz) of white sugarpaste and trim neatly around the edges.

24 The car is now covered with paste, so all that is needed is to finish the details. Make a template for the headlights from your source material and cut

them from 20g (¾oz) of white sugarpaste. Attach to the bonnet of the car with edible glue.

25 Work a small amount of white vegetable fat into approximately 25g (1oz) of Daffodil paste, then extrude a string of paste using the small, round disc in the sugar shaper. Attach to the front of the car, following a line running up to the front edge of the doors, up to the corner (where the wing mirrors will be) and around in a curve, separating the bonnet section from the bumper section. Do the same around headlights.

26 Use the same method as step 25 with Black MMP and use this paste to outline the windows, windscreen and black roof section.

27 Use 25g (1oz) of Black MMP to make the front and back bumpers. Tuck the sides of the bumper around and into the wheel wells.

28 For each wheel you will need approximately around 50g (1¾oz) of Black MMP. Add a small amount of white vegetable fat to each ball and knead it in well. Drop it into the wheel mould,

press firmly and cut off the excess from the back using the mini palette knife. Slightly squeeze the sides of the mould first, then turn it upside down and tap the base with the handle of the mini palette knife until the wheel drops out. Make four.

29 Make the wing mirrors from the remnants of Black MMP and use a strand of spaghetti to attach them to the corner of the door/window. Use edible glue for extra support.

30 Finish the car by painting the roof, side panel, headlights and the spokes of the wheels with edible silver paint.

31 Finish the car by adding the brake lights. To make these, colour a small pinch of white sugarpaste with Poppy paste colour. Shape into two short sausages, flatten and use a craft knife to neaten the edges. Attach to the car using edible glue.

32 Finish the cake by making a few grass tufts from the remnants of the paste used on the base. Attach these around the car using edible glue.

motorbike

The motorbike is a relatively complicated design but if you follow the carving carefully you will master it. It is well worth the effort and if you do go wrong with some of the carving, just mix the cake with some buttercream and stick it back on!

Edibles

25cm (10") square sponge cake

500g (1lb 1½oz) vanilla buttercream

2kg (4lb 6½oz) sugarpaste: white

SK Mexican Modelling Paste (MMP): 500g
(1lb 1½oz) Black, 1kg (2lb 3¼oz) White

SK Paste Food Colours: Bluebell, Daffodil,
Forest Green, Poinsettia, Vine

SK Edible Metallic Paint: Silver

Clear alcohol (e.g. gin or vodka)

Equipment

Basic equipment (see pages 6 to 9)

30.5cm x 35.5cm (12" x 14") rectangular
cake drum

4cm and 6cm (1½" and 2½") round
cutters

Sponge, new and sterilised in boiling water

SK Great Impressions Teddy Bear Texture
Mat

Motorbike template (see page 93)

Slices: approximately 35

1 Colour 300g (10½oz) of white sugarpaste with a small amount of Bluebell paste colour to make a sky blue. Dampen the cake drum with cooled, boiled water, roll out the paste and cover the top half of the drum. Make a light colour wash by mixing Bluebell paste colour with clear alcohol and use the sponge to apply the colour to the light blue paste, giving a natural sky effect. Pat the sponge lightly onto a piece of kitchen roll first so you don't apply too much colour.

2 Colour 100g (3½oz) of white sugarpaste with Forest Green paste colour. Roll out and cover the bottom half of the cake drum.

3 Colour 75g (2½oz) of sugarpaste using Vine paste colour, roll into a sausage shape and flatten with the texture mat to give the effect of vegetation. Attach to the cake drum, covering the join between the sky and grass. Press with a flower shaping tool to give depth. Leave to dry.

4 Place the cake onto a spare cake drum. Trim off the top of the cake to make it roughly flat. Turn the cake over and, using the motorbike template, cut out the shape using the small knife. Cut around the template using the knife and cut away the cake. For the more intricate parts of the template, use the mini palette knife to cut guidelines before shaping the cake.

5 Following the guidelines marked on the cake from the template, start trimming and cutting the motorbike shape, leaving the guidelines in place to work from.

6 Keep the template to hand so you can also use this for reference when making areas shallower – parts that are further away such as the area around the rider's foot and the section in front of the rider's chest should be shallow.

7 Soften the cut edges of the cake using the mini palette knife, then use this to finish trimming and neatening the carving you have achieved.

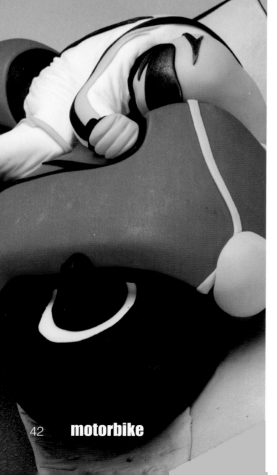

8 Cover the biker section with a thin layer of buttercream.

9 Mould small pieces of MMP to raise up the features of the biker before you cover the whole cake.

10 Cover the entire cake with a thin layer of buttercream. Roll out 500g (1lb 1½oz) of white sugarpaste and cover the whole cake. Carefully use the flower shaping tool to indent the shapes you have just cut. This layer will keep crumbs away from the finished design.

11 Start decorating the cake by covering the wheels with 300g (10½oz) of Black MMP. The front wheel is fairly straightforward, but the back wheel needs to be covered along with the underside of the seating section and the area around the engine and exhaust. To add further detail to the wheels, use the largest circle cutter to cut out the centre of the wheels and remove the paste. Cut a smaller circle from this paste to make a small black disc. Mark this with curved lines coming from the centre.

12 Use the large and small circle

cutters again to cut a ring of White MMP for each wheel and place this inside the tyre. Slot the black disc into this.

13 Colour 1kg (2lb 3¼oz) of white sugarpaste with Poinsettia paste food colour to make a bright red. Carefully dampen the relevant area on the motorbike with cooled, boiled water and apply the paste to the prepared areas, i.e. the body of the motorbike, the seat and the front section. Smooth the paste using a pad of the same paste, then with a craft knife, cut away the red paste neatly to leave straight lines. Be as neat as you can when cutting the paste away but don't worry too much if the finish isn't perfect as the edges will be covered. Tuck the paste in around the top and bottom of the motorbike. Once you are happy with the neatened edges, leave to dry (this makes the next part of the process easier).

14 Following the same principles, cover the whole of the biker with 500g (1lb 1½oz) of White MMP, cutting and trimming neatly up against the red paste using the craft knife. Use the pointed end of the flower shaping tool to help neaten the edges and to add creases in the trousers

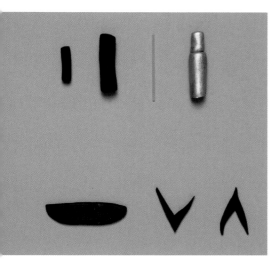

and around the sleeve. End the arm covering at the wrist.

15 Shape a pinch of Black MMP into a small disc, then attach this to the bike just in front of the end of the arm. Insert a short strand of spaghetti into the centre of this for the handlebar and cover with Black MMP.

16 Colour 300g (10½oz) of White MMP with Vine paste colour. Shape a hand and attach it to the motorbike handle and the end of the arm. Use the remaining paste to cover the helmet and cut stripes to add to the arms, back and leg of the biker. The remnants can be used on the front of the bike to add detail.

17 Add flashes to the biker's leathers and helmet using Black MMP and a ribbon cutter, then make the visor. Attach all the detailing in place using edible glue.

18 Use the remaining Black MMP to make the engine parts, the pipe work around the front of the bike, the axel and the exhausts. Attach in place with edible glue.

19 Finish the bike by painting the exhaust with edible silver paint.

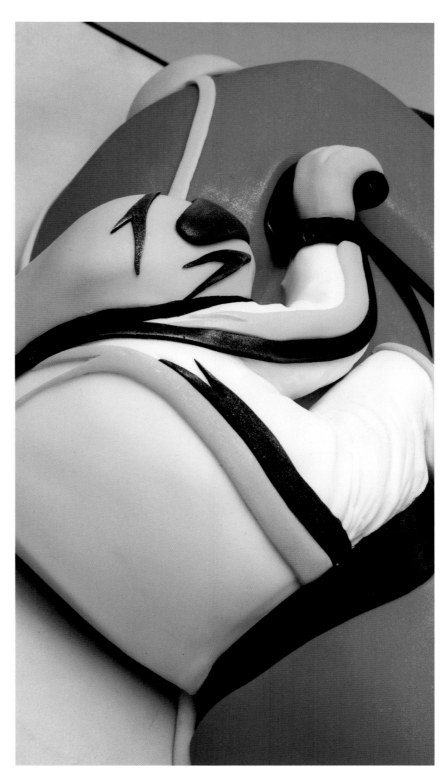

tankard

Edibles

23cm (9") square cake

300g (10½oz) buttercream

3kg (6lb 9¾oz) sugarpaste: white

300g (10½oz) SK Mexican Modelling
Paste (MMP): White

50g (1¾oz) SK Instant Mix Royal Icing

SK Paste Food Colours: Bluebell, Jet
Black

SK Edible Metallic Paint: Silver

White vegetable fat

Equipment

Basic equipment (see pages 6 to 9)

20cm (8") oval cake drum

8cm and 10cm (3" and 4") circle cutters

Bubbles texture mat (SA)

Key and scroll templates (see page 93)

Slices: approximately 35

Not as intoxicating as a real
tankard of beer – I think this
version tastes much better!

1 Use the cake marker to trim the top of the cake so that it is level and flat. Turn the cake over.

2 Indent the cake with the circle cutters, one of each size, keeping the circles neatly to one side.

3 Do the same at the other side of the cake, ensuring you have positioned the circles so you can cut four circles altogether, two large and two small. Push the cutters into the cake (they won't go all the way through).

4 Using a sharp knife, cut away the cake around the circles that you have just cut.

5 Trim away the brown crust of the cake, leaving four neat mini circle cakes.

6 Stack the cakes on top of each other and neaten the sides, then trim the top to a maximum height of 18cm (7").

7 Stick the cakes together using buttercream then push two food grade dowels down through the length to support the stack. Trim the dowels to the height of the cake by marking them with a scalpel, removing then cutting them to size. Re-insert the dowels then place the cake stack on the spare cake drum.

8 Leaving the bottom 2.5cm (1") untrimmed, trim the rest of the cake down to a maximum of 10cm (4") in diameter at the top of the cake using a small, sharp knife and a mini palette knife. Cover the whole cake with a thin layer of buttercream.

9 Colour 1.5kg (3lb 5oz) of sugarpaste with a very small amount of Jet Black paste colour to make a very light grey colour. Roll out using a large rolling pin

then trim the top and bottom of the paste straight using a pizza wheel.

10 Carefully lift the paste and wrap it around the cake, using the cake smoothers to assist you. Trim the paste at the back of the cake using the small, sharp knife, then smooth the paste back again and polish out any dents or finger marks with a pad of paste. Trim the top of the paste level with the cake.

11 Dampen the 20cm (8") oval cake drum with cooled, boiled water. Colour the remaining sugarpaste with Bluebell paste colour. Roll out the pale blue paste then place the bubbles texture mat on top of the sugarpaste and roll over firmly. Gently remove the mat and carefully transfer the paste to the cake drum, taking care not to trap any air bubbles underneath. Trim and neaten the edge. Place the cake onto the prepared cake drum.

12 Colour 200g (7¼oz) of the White MMP light grey in the same way as for the sugarpaste. Add a little white vegetable fat to 50g (1¾oz) of the paste to soften it then extrude the paste through the sugar

shaper to create a long sausage. Attach the sausage around the base of the cake, around the top of the lower part and around the lip of the tankard. Secure in place with edible glue.

13 Shape the remaining White MMP into the froth to go on top of the tankard. Pinch off a little to make the drips down the side of the tankard, shape into three teardrops and attach to in place with edible glue. Shape the remaining paste into a circle and flatten with your thumbs and the flat end of the flower shaping tool. Place on the top of the tankard and flatten more if needed.

14 Prepare the template on tracing paper. Roll out 50g (1¾oz) of the grey MMP and cut out the key and scroll carefully using a craft knife. Neaten the edge of the key using the flower shaping tool. Cut out the number freehand and attach to the front of the key using edible glue. Attach the key to the front of the tankard with the scroll on top.

15 Make up the royal icing and add a tiny amount of Jet Black paste colour

TIP

If you have a number cutter set you can use this to cut out the number on the key.

to make the same shade as the tankard. Place the icing into a piping bag with a no. 1 nozzle and pipe your chosen inscription onto the scroll.

16 Shape the remaining grey modelling paste into a long teardrop for the handle. Trim the paste to size, coil the top end and bend the other end into a slight S shape. Make a cut at the bottom end and separate the paste. Attach to the side of the tankard using edible glue and support it in place until it holds firm. Use the remaining off-cuts of paste to make tiny pearls decreasing in size. Attach to the handle. Allow the tankard to dry.

17 Using a large paintbrush, paint the whole tankard with edible silver paint then leave to dry.

baseball boots

Edibles

25.5cm (10") square cake

4kg (8lb 13¼oz) sugarpaste: white

225g (8oz) buttercream

SK Paste Food Colours: Chestnut, Hydrangea, Jet Black, Vine

300g (10½oz) SK Mexican Modelling Paste (MMP): Black

SK Edible Metallic Paint: Silver

SK Edible Glue

White vegetable fat

Equipment

Basic equipment (see pages 6 to 9)

Boot template (see page 94)

Slices: approximately 45

I love these boots, they never seem to go out of fashion. I remember having a pair – mine were tartan as a tribute to the Bay City Rollers!

1 Cut the cake in half. Cut and shape both boots at the same time and once you have shaped both, wrap one in cling film while you are working on the other cake – this will stop it drying out until you are ready to cover it. Place the template onto the cake and cut around it using a sharp knife (you can use a large or small knife, whichever you prefer).

2 Cut the instep of the boot, remembering that on the second boot you must do this on the opposite side to the first, otherwise you will end up with two shoes for the same foot! I find this is easiest to do using a mini palette knife as it is small and easy to manipulate.

3 To shape the front of the boot, remove the corners first then shape and trim the cake carefully. Work your way up the front of the boot, trimming and shaping the cake a little at a time.

4 Shape the back of the boot, cutting away more of the central area to create the ankle shape.

5 Carve the sides of the boot, creating slight curves so the front and back sections you have worked on blend in with the sides smoothly.

6 Trim the base of the boot to curve the lower edge inwards slightly.

7 Repeat the same instructions to create the second boot.

8 Once you have carved a left and right boot, decorate them one at a time and wrap the other in cling film to keep the cake fresh. Cover the boot with a thin layer of buttercream, then roll out 450g (1lb) of white sugarpaste and cover the cake. Use your hands to smooth the paste onto the cake then cut off any excess. Use a pad

of paste to smooth the surface and remove any cracks or creases. This layer will keep the cake moist whilst you work on it and will also stop any crumbs spoiling the finish.

9 Roll approximately 200g (7¼oz) of white sugarpaste into a long sausage. Flatten with the rolling pin and roll out to around 4mm (1/8") thick and 2.5cm (1") wide. Attach around the bottom of the boot.

TIP

If you haven't made the sausage long enough to do it in one piece, don't worry – you can attach it in two pieces, joining them at the heel and toe. Use edible glue to attach it in place.

10 Shape the semicircular toecap from approximately 50g (1¾oz) of white sugarpaste. Roll out the paste, then roll the ribbed rolling pin over the paste in one direction followed by the other direction to create a criss-cross pattern. Place over the toe of the boot, 5cm (2") from the front, and attach with edible glue. Use a craft knife to trim away any excess paste at the front. Smooth the join with the flower shaping tool.

11 Colour 100g (3½oz) of white sugarpaste with Chestnut paste colour to make the tongue of the boot. Roll out the paste to approximately 12cm (5") in length and 5cm (2") in width. Shape one end into a curve and keep the other end square. Place the square end up to the toe of the boot and secure the tongue in place with edible glue. Support the length extending from the top of the boot with a ball of kitchen towel until dry.

12 Cut a template for the side of the boot using a sheet of greaseproof paper. Wrap this around the boot over the area to be covered, then use a pencil to mark the outline required for one side of the boot on the paper. The boot side overlaps the front by approximately 5mm (1/8") and raises up towards ankle section of the boot by 2.5cm (1"). Both sides of the boot will be made from the same template.

13 Colour 2kg (4lb 6½oz) of white sugarpaste with Vine paste colour – this is enough to cover both boots so keep any paste that you are not using sealed in a polythene bag to prevent it from drying out. Roll out 500g (1lb 1½oz) of the Vine paste and cut out the boot

shape using the template and a craft knife, taking care not to pull the paste as you work. Attach to the boot using edible glue. Smooth the surface with a pad of paste, then trim at the back so the covering ends neatly down the centre. Cut the other side in the same way and create a neat join at the back. Support the back of the boot with the kitchen towel if necessary.

14 Use a stitching wheel to make two rows of stitching around the edge of the green paste. Cut out six eyelets for the laces with a mini circle cutter and use a ruler to make sure they are the same distance apart all the way down.

15 Colour 30g (1oz) of White MMP with Hydrangea paste colour, then knead in a little white vegetable fat to soften the paste. Extrude the sugarpaste through the sugar shaper using the larger of the single-hole discs. Attach this using edible glue to the top edge of the boot sides and around the top. Make another string of paste in the same way and join the two at the back of the boot top. With the remaining paste, cut a strip of paste using a ribbon cutter set to a width of approximately 1.2cm (½"). Run the stitching wheel up both sides of this

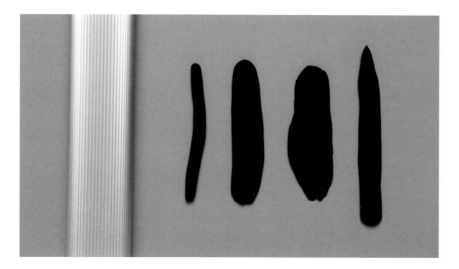

ribbon then loop the top over and cut off the excess paste. (The loop should support itself but you can use a small roll of kitchen towel if required.) Secure in place with edible glue, covering the join at the top of the boot.

16 Fit the sugar shaper with the smallest single-hole disc. Soften 25g (1oz) of White MMP with white vegetable fat then extrude it through the sugar shaper and coil small lengths of the paste around the eyelet holes. Secure with edible glue, then paint with edible silver paint.

17 Roll the remaining White MMP into a sausage and flatten. Texture with a ribbed rolling pin then using the ribbon cutter, cut a strip 2cm (¾") wide. Cut to 12.5cm (5") long and wrap around the front of the toe area, attaching with edible glue. Trim the ends so they slope downwards.

18 To make the laces roll out lengths of Black MMP, texture with the ribbed rolling pin and trim to 1.5cm (½") wide with the ribbon cutter. Accentuate the ribbing using the pointed end of the flower shaping tool. Cut the laces to approximately 5cm (2") in length, pinch one end slightly and thread it into the topmost left-hand eyelet.

Allow the lace to drape across towards the second eyelet down on the right-hand side. Flatten the lace onto the tongue and attach with edible glue. Trim off the excess and flatten the end slightly so it looks like it is going under the boot. Continue with the right-hand lace leading to the second eyelet down on the left-hand side so that they cross over in the middle. Continue the pattern all the way down to the bottom.

19 Make a lace in the same way for the bottom but pinch both ends this time and tuck into both the bottom eyelets.

20 Roll out the remaining Black MMP and cut a ribbon to run around the top of the white base of the boot, approximately 1cm (³/₈") wide. Use the same paste to make flashes to decorate the boot, cutting out the shapes you require with a craft knife.

TIP

You could make up your own pattern here or put in the recipient's initials or name.

burger

Edibles

2 x 17.5cm (7") round cakes (one needs
to be at least 12.5cm (5") deep)

300g (10½oz) buttercream

Sugarpaste: 2kg (4lb 6½oz) celebration
(cream), 1kg (2lb 3¼oz) dark brown

SK Mexican Modelling Paste (MMP): 100g
(3½oz) Black, 300g (10½oz) White

200g (7¼oz) SK Sugar Florist Paste (SFP):
Cream

500g (1lb 1½oz) SK Marzipan

SK Dust Food Colours: Chestnut,
Marigold, Poinsettia, Vine

SK Metallic Lustre Dust Food Colour:
Snowflake

SK Paste Food Colours: Bulrush,
Chestnut, Cream, Jet Black

SK Instant Mix Royal Icing (small
amount)

Equipment

Basic equipment (see
pages 6 to 9)

23cm (9") round cake drum

15cm (6") round cake card

SK Great Impressions Teddy
Bear Texture Mat

Frilling tool (OCT)

Slices: approximately 45

Such an amusing cake to make
for the burger-mad man in your life!

1 Use the cake marker to mark a line halfway up the side of the deep cake.

2 Cut the deep cake into two equal halves with a large, serrated knife. Follow the scribed line on the cake to ensure both halves are even.

3 Take a mini palette knife and start to trim the edges of the cake, beginning the curved shape of the top bun.

4 Continue to work around the cake, trimming away small pieces at a time to give the top of the cake an even, curved shape.

5 Trim the other cake into a bun shape, this time making it less curved for the bottom bun.

6 Trim the second, shallower cake to create the burger. Shape the edges in the same way as for the bun, but this time flip it over and shape again to make the top and bottom even.

7 Cut the two bun cakes in half and fill with buttercream, then cover the surface with buttercream. Cover with cream sugarpaste, then trim away any excess paste and tuck the edges under slightly. Reserve the paste trimmings for later.

8 Indent the top bun with the tip of the frilling tool in several places. Make tiny balls of remnant paste for the sesame seeds on the bun and attach in place with dots of royal icing. Dust the bun with Chestnut dust colour mixed with a little Snowflake lustre dust to give some sparkle. When applying the dust the top bun should be darker on top and lighter down the sides, whereas the base bun should be dusted darker on the sides graduating to a light colour at the top.

9 Crinkle a piece of kitchen foil up to make a support for the wrapper, making the base of the support flat for the bun to sit on. Roll out the Cream SFP very thinly into a large square, use a stitching wheel to mark to a neat square around the edge, then use a pizza wheel to completely cut through the paste just outside this line. This gives the wrapper a perforated look. Drape over the kitchen foil to dry.

10 Place the base bun cake onto the wrapper whilst it is still on the foil and leave to dry.

11 Colour the remnants of the ivory sugarpaste with Chestnut paste colour and use this to cover the 23cm (9") cake drum. Trim neatly around the edge and leave to dry.

12 Once the burger wrapper is dry, push away the foil and lift the wrapper and bun base onto the prepared cake drum. Position in the centre of the drum and secure in place with a little royal icing.

13 Cover the remaining cake with a thin layer of buttercream. Cover the cake with the dark brown sugarpaste and tuck the edges of the paste underneath. Use the teddy texture mat to give a squiggly, slightly grainy effect to resemble a real burger. Place this cake onto the 15cm (6") cake card to give a little support.

14 Insert the cake dowels into the base bun, score level with the top, remove and cut to size. Re-insert the dowels into the cake then place the burger cake onto the bun, securing in place with a little royal icing.

15 Prepare the lettuce leaves by colouring approximately half the marzipan with Vine dust food colour. The heat from your hands will warm up and soften the marzipan so once the colour is blended in, leave the marzipan to cool down to room temperature in a sealed plastic food bag. Once the consistency has returned to normal, form pieces of paste into rough oval shapes and roll quite thinly using the small rolling pin. Place on a foam pad and use a cocktail stick or frilling tool to frill and stretch the marzipan a little, resembling a lettuce leaf. Make several leaves and arrange on the burger cake, draping them slightly over the edge.

16 Continue by making the vegetables for the burger, colouring the marzipan in small amounts as needed. Use Marigold to make orange marzipan for the slices of orange pepper, and Poinsettia for the red pepper. Drape the pepper pieces onto the lettuce, making sure they are towards the edges so will be seen when the top bun is in position. Use a small amount of White MMP to make a few onion slices and arrange around the edges. Place a few more marzipan lettuce leaves on top to make the garnish look well packed.

17 To make the whole tomato slice, colour a small amount of marzipan a lighter red/pink, roll out and cut a circle for the centre of the tomato. Darken the remnants to a deeper red for the outer section of the tomato. Roll out and cut a strip using the ribbon cutter. Wrap this around the pink centre and use edible glue to stick the two together. Make the seeds from the natural marzipan, roll into

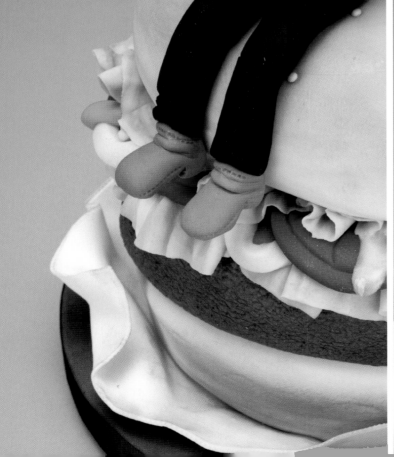
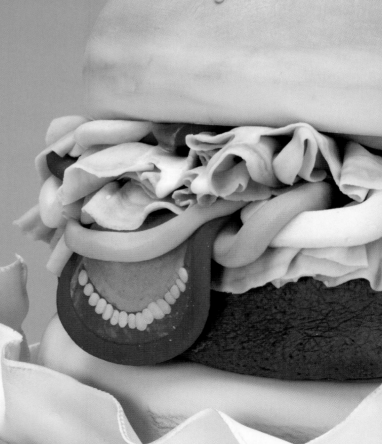

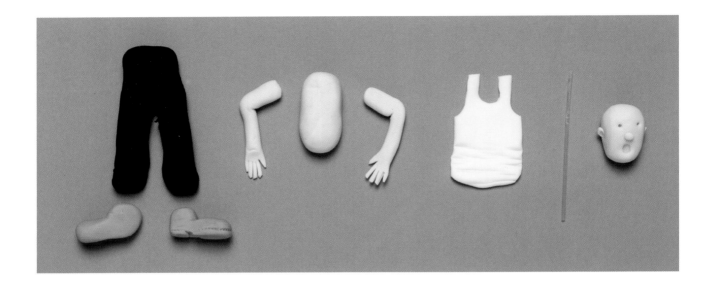

tiny balls and flatten along the join. Drape this on top of the lettuce already on the burger, making sure that it can be seen by allowing it to trail down the outside.

18 Drizzle a little thin royal icing sparingly over the garnish to look like burger sauce, then place the top bun over the burger filling, using thicker royal icing to secure it in place.

19 Make the mini burger that the man is holding first so that it can be left to dry whilst you make him. Use pinches of paste (approximately 10g/¼oz) for each component, i.e. two buns, a burger and a tiny lettuce leaf. Secure together with tiny dots of royal icing.

20 For the man's trousers, roll a sausage of Black MMP then slice in half lengthways, but only cut ¾ down the length so the legs are still joined at the top. Soften the cut edge and shape the legs with your fingers. Bend the top part over for the waist and use the pointed end of a flower shaping tool to mark creases at the crotch area and around the base of the trouser legs. Sit the legs on the side of

the burger bun and secure with royal icing. For extra support you may wish to push a spaghetti strand down through the waist and into the cake (remember to remove this before the cake is eaten).

21 Colour 100g (3½oz) of White MMP with Chestnut paste colour to give a light beige tone. Model the head into a pear shape, indent the mouth with the small end of the bone tool, then add the ears and nose. Shape the body and arms from the same paste. Secure the body to the waist using edible glue and support by pushing a spaghetti strand through the neck and down into the trousers, leaving a small amount of the strand protruding to assist in securing the head. Attach the head in the same way. Bend the arms at right angles and attach to the body using a tiny strand of spaghetti and edible glue. Support the arms using kitchen roll tucked underneath the elbows.

22 Position the burger in the hands and secure with royal icing. Support this with folded kitchen roll between the burger and the legs until the whole section is dry – this will take a couple of hours but it is best to

leave it overnight if possible. Remove the paper from under the arms and burger.

23 Roll out 50g (1¾oz) of White MMP and carefully cut out the vest in two parts, front and back. Carefully slip the front section between the body and the burger and secure to the body using edible glue. Using the flower shaping tool, mark creases on the vest around the arms and bottom. Do the same with the back, joining the two sections together at the shoulders.

24 Finish the figure off by adding two black eyes and black hair. To make the hair, knead some white vegetable fat into the remnants of Black MMP, extrude this through the sugar shaper with the multi-hole disc and attach the strands to the head using edible glue.

25 Finally, make the shoes from 30g (1oz) of Chestnut coloured MMP. Shape the paste into two ovals then use the flower shaping tool to shape and indent creases along the top. Attach to the legs using strands of spaghetti and dots of royal icing. Press into place and hold until secure.

mini burgers

These are made from two cupcakes each, shaped slightly using the mini palette knife then covered in sugarpaste in the same way as for the large cake. The salad filling is made from marzipan in the same way as the main cake, and the burger is made from a small round of marzipan coloured with Bulrush paste colour or a piece of dark brown sugarpaste. Use a piece of dry spaghetti to hold the mini burger together.

camper van

I was born a little too late to be a hippy or to appreciate the Beach Boys first time round, but I think there is a little flower power and 'beach bum' in all of us!

Edibles

25.5cm (10") square sponge cake

250g (8¾oz) buttercream

3kg (6lb 9¾oz) sugarpaste: white

SK Mexican Modelling Paste (MMP): 200g (7¼oz) Black, 400g (14¼oz) White

100g (3½oz) SK Sugar Florist Paste (SFP): White

Small amount SK Instant Mix Royal Icing

SK Paste Food Colours: Chestnut, Fern, Fuchsia, Gentian, Vine, Violet

SK Edible Metallic Paint: Silver

Equipment

Basic equipment (see pages 6 to 9)

25.5cm (10") square cake drum

SK Great Impressions Teddy Bear Texture Mat

SK Great Impressions Wheel Mould: small

Camper van templates (see page 94 or make your own from source material)

Surfboard template (see page 94)

Blossom plunger cutter (PME)

Five-petal blossom cutter (OCT)

Slices: approximately 45

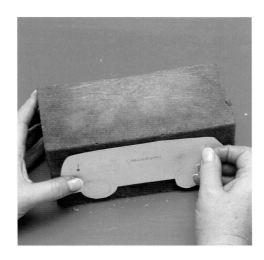

1 Cut the cake into two oblongs measuring 25.5cm x 15.5cm (10" x 6") and 25.5cm x 10cm (10" x 4"). Cover the larger section with cling film to keep it moist until required. Take the smaller oblong, cut it in half horizontally to make two shallow 25.5cm x 10cm (10" x 4") oblongs and separate the cakes. This cake will be used as the land that the camper van is placed on. Place on the cake drum and trim around the cake, taking merely a sliver off two sides, but trimming the other two and taking the corner off to make a smooth curve.

2 Cover the cake with a thin layer of buttercream. Colour 500g (1lb 1½oz) of sugarpaste with a tiny amount of Chestnut paste colour, roll out fairly thinly then cover the cake. Smooth the paste around the shape of the cake.

3 Make the grass from 400g (14¼oz) of white sugarpaste coloured with Fern paste colour. Roll out the paste fairly thickly and before you cover the cake, push one side in to squash the edge of the paste a little. Lay this side over the curved edge of the cake but don't allow it to completely cover the side of the cake as you still need to see the edge of the land. Allow it to be lumpy and bumpy like the top of a cliff or a field and emboss with the texture mat to make it look like grass. If you want to make some little hillocks, push some of the green paste through a sieve, scrape off with a mini palette knife and attach to the cake with edible glue.

4 Make the sea and waves from 200g (7¼oz) of white sugarpaste coloured very slightly with a little Gentian paste colour. Cover the cake drum with this, allowing the paste to ripple around the curve of the

land. Accentuate the rippled effect with the flower shaping tool. Once this is dry, paint the waves with a little white royal icing and a little royal icing tinged with Gentian paste colour to create a realistic effect.

5 Carve the camper van from the remaining cake. Make a template for the side of a camper van (see the Microcar project on page 34 for instructions on making templates from source material), place the template up against the cake and pin it in place using sterilised glass-headed pins.

TIP

Make sure you count the pins out and back again so that there is no chance they can get into the cake. If you don't want to use pins you could use cocktail sticks to hold the template in place.

6 Take a large, sharp knife and cut around your template, making sure you don't undercut the shape.

7 Using the mini palette knife, cut out the wheel arches and where the wheels will be, then mark a line across the side of the camper van at the point where the coloured body work changes to white. (You will be able to find this from your source material or follow the templates provided.) Don't trim too far into the wheel arches as you will need sufficient cake under the camper to support it.

8 Trim away the sides of the camper van down to the line you have just marked to narrow the top part only.

9 Use the mini palette knife to start trimming the front section of the camper van, taking off a little at a time to achieve the curved shape. Work your way around the camper van, trimming off the straight edges at an angle to soften the whole shape.

10 Finish trimming the front of the camper van around the base of the cake. Take care not to go too far – there comes a point where you have to stop and be satisfied with the shape you have created!

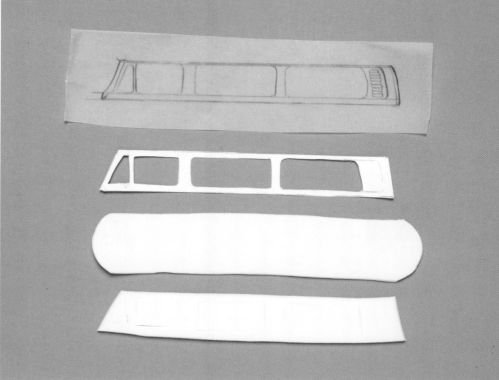

11 Cover the cake with a thin layer of buttercream, then cover with 500g (1lb 1½oz) of white sugarpaste. Roll out the paste quite thinly and smooth it over the shape of the cake. This will keep crumbs at bay and give you a smooth working surface on which to finish your camper. Whilst the paste is still soft, use the pointed end of a flower shaping tool to mark the paste with guidelines for the sections of the camper, using the templates provided or your own. You can mark as much or as little as you like to aid your design. Make sure you mark the front of the camper van and make a template of the curve so you can recreate it in green paste.

12 Cut a thin strip from approximately 100g (3½oz) of Black MMP to go around the base of the cake. The strip needs to be as deep as the wheel arches and should be narrow as it must fit under the bumper. Secure in place with edible glue.

13 Colour 1kg (2lb 3¼oz) of white sugarpaste with Vine paste colour. This is enough to cover the whole cake so seal any paste you aren't using in a plastic food bag to stop it drying out.

14 Using the templates provided (which you may need to enlarge to fit your cake) or your own templates made from source material, cut out the sections of the camper van starting with the long, Vine green side panel. Cut the green sections slightly thicker than the white sections so they stand out a little, accentuating the bottom-heavy appearance of the camper van. Secure the bodywork in place with edible glue, then use a pad of paste to smooth the surface. Trim around the wheel arch and neaten.

15 Make the door panel next in the same way. Smooth around the wheel arch as before and add a tiny white handle to the door.

16 Cut the green sections for the front of the camper using the template you made earlier. Smooth the surface with a pad of paste, trim the curve carefully then smooth the edge with the flower shaping tool to make sure you have a sharp edge.

17 Continue working around the camper van, fitting the panels along the opposite side and the boot.

18 The window sections and roof are all cut from White MMP. Start by making the template for the side windows: roll out approximately 75g (2½oz) of MMP thinner than the green paste, then place the template on top and cut around it using a pizza wheel. Use the scalpel to mark where the windows will be cut out, then remove the template and finish cutting the windows out, making them as neat as you can. Don't take too long over this as the paste will be drying as you work. Attach to the camper using edible glue. Repeat on the opposite side.

19 Follow the same method for the front and back windows; you will need 50g (1¾oz) for each window.

20 Cut a template for the roof and a 'v' shape for the front bonnet. Roll out 100g (3½oz) of White MMP for the roof section, smooth the curves on the piece before you slot it in, then smooth with a pad of paste to flatten the roof slightly, allowing it to fit in the slot and fill any gaps. Roll out the remnants of paste and make the 'v' shape for the bonnet. Smooth into place with a pad of paste.

21 Roll 25g (1oz) of White MMP into a long sausage, using two cake smoothers to get an even shape, then cut to length for the roof rack. Secure in place with edible glue.

22 Make the headlamps and front lights from pinches of White MMP and secure in place.

23 Roll out 75g (2½oz) of White MMP quite thickly into a long strip. Using the ribbon cutter, cut a strip approximately 1cm (³/₈") wide. Cut this into sections to run around the base of the bodywork for the front and back bumpers and the side runners. Secure in place using edible glue.

24 Add a little white vegetable fat to the remaining Black MMP and split into four equal balls (approximately 50g/1¾oz each) to make the wheels. Roll each piece into a smooth ball, drop it into the mould and press it in firmly. Smooth the back flat. Turn the mould over and use the handle of the mini palette knife to pat the base of the mould until the wheel drops out. Place each wheel into a wheel arch and secure with edible glue.

25 Soften 25g (1oz) of White MMP with white vegetable fat then extrude through the sugar shaper, creating a long, thin string of paste. Use this string to neaten around the edge of the windows, the 'v' section of the front bonnet and the join of the roof. Use the remnants of this paste to make two small wing mirrors. Attach these using edible glue and a strand of spaghetti.

26 Paint the windows, headlamps, wing mirrors and spokes of the wheels with edible silver paint.

27 Knead the White SFP and roll to approximately 3mm (¹/₈") deep. Using the pizza wheel and surfboard template, cut out two boards. Place on a surface dusted with cornflour to dry. Once dry, place one on top of the camper and lean one up against it.

28 Finish the cake by decorating the side of the camper van and surfboard with pink blossoms and purple hibiscus flowers. To make the blossoms, colour the remnants of SFP with a little Fuchsia paste colour, roll out the paste and cut out several flowers using the blossom plunger cutter.

29 To make the purple hibiscus flowers, roll out some Violet coloured SFP and cut out several five-petal blossoms using a larger cutter. Cut each petal out, cut off the point of the petal and indent twice using the flower shaping tool, then stick the petals back together. To make the stamens add a pinch of white to some remnant Violet paste, roll into a long cone, flatten the wider end, then use a craft knife to cut slits along the flattened end to make it look frizzy.

30 Using remnants of the green paste used for the side of the camper, roll out and cut the green flashes for the surfboard using the pizza wheel. They can be as broad or as narrow as you wish. Secure with edible glue. Pipe the 'surf dude' lettering onto the surfboard using a small amount of royal icing coloured with a little Violet paste colour in a piping bag with a no. 1 piping nozzle.

31 Secure the decoration to the van and surfboards with edible glue.

camper van cupcakes

These cupcakes are simple to make: cover with a swirl of buttercream, place a disc of green sugarpaste on the top then decorate with flowers in the same way as for the camper van.

mad professor

I love the concept of this wacky cake –
turning all our rubbish into jelly beans.
I know my son Charlie would definitely
have this installed in his bedroom!

Edibles

15cm (6") square cake

2 x 10cm (4") round cakes*

3kg (6lb 9¾oz) sugarpaste: white

500g (1lb 1½oz) SK Mexican Modelling Paste (MMP): White

SK Sugar Florist Paste: 50g (1¾oz) Black, 100g (3½oz) White

300g (10½oz) SK Instant Mix Royal Icing

SK Paste Food Colours: Berberis, Bluebell, Bulrush, Chestnut, Daffodil, Fuchsia, Gentian, Jet Black, Marigold, Poppy, Violet

SK Edible Metallic Paint: Silver

SK Leaf Gelatine

White vegetable fat

Equipment

Basic equipment (see pages 6 to 9)

23cm (9") square cake drum

5cm (2") round cake card**

6 mini posy picks

50cm (19½") aluminium craft wire (LC)

Micro circle cutter (KB)

*Use the same quantity of cake mix as for a 15cm (6") round cake (see pages 14 to 15).

**Most cake decorating suppliers don't sell cake cards this small, so you may have to cut this from a larger size.

Slices: approximately 25

1 Colour 500g (1lb 1½oz) of white sugarpaste with a tiny dot of Jet Black paste colour. Roll out the paste, cover the cake drum and smooth with cake smoothers to create a blemish-free surface. Use a ruler and the pointed end of the flower veining tool to mark lines across the paste at a diagonal angle, measuring the distance between the lines to keep it the same. Mark more lines at 90 degrees to the first lines to create the tile effect on the floor. Make the lines fairly deep.

2 Place a no. 1 nozzle into a piping bag and fill with royal icing coloured to a slightly darker grey shade than the floor tiles. Pipe a line of royal icing into each of the grooves, then flatten and smooth the royal icing with your finger to resemble grouting. Don't worry if it smudges slightly, it will add to the effect!

3 Sandwich the round cakes together with buttercream, then start carving the cakes into a 10cm (4") ball shape for the jelly bean machine following steps 2 and 3 of the Alien cake (see page 31).

4 Carve the control centre that the jelly bean machine sits on from the square cake. Using the ruler, measure 2.5cm (1") in from the outer corner on each side. Mark a line from this point to the back corner using a sharp knife, creating a very long triangular shape, then cut this triangle off each side to make a trapezium. The wide end will be the back of the control centre.

5 Turn the cake onto its front end (the narrower end) then use the side marker to mark two lines across the cake, one at 5cm (2") and one at 7.5cm (3") from the end.

6 Place the cake flat again with the narrow end closest to you. Cut off the triangle of cake from the first line down at an angle to the bottom front edge to give the control centre a slanted front.

7 Measure 1cm (³/₈") down from the second line you marked, then cut across at this level with a sharp knife.

8 Cut downwards along the marked line to cut this front section out.

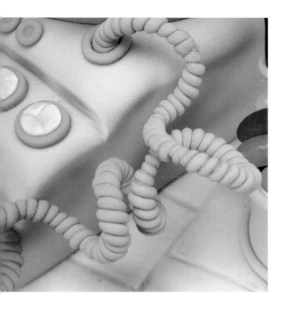

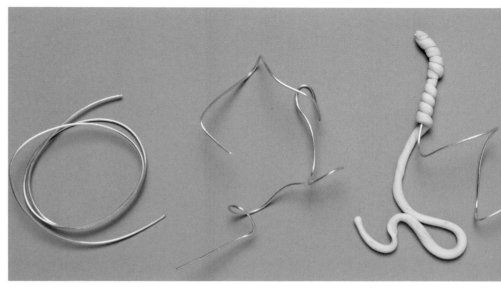

9 Slice the top of the control centre off, ensuring it is completely flat.

10 Finish the control centre by trimming off the edges using the mini palette knife. Work your way round the centre, taking off just a sliver of cake.

11 Cover the whole cake with a layer of buttercream. Colour 250g (8¾oz) of sugarpaste with a little Berberis and cover the cake with this. Smooth the paste into the control panel section, keeping the angle of the step cut into the cake. Once dry, place centrally on the prepared cake drum. Push two dowels down through the cake, mark level with the top of the cake and remove. Use a craft knife to cut the dowels to size then re-insert them into the cake.

12 Place the ball cake onto a 5cm (2") round cake card. Cover the cake with buttercream then colour 400g (14¼oz) of sugarpaste with Daffodil paste colour to make a bright yellow. Place the cake on top of the control centre, then polish the surface with a pad of paste to remove any finger marks. Leave to dry.

13 Divide the Black MMP in two and make two cone shapes, one for the rubbish going in and one for the jelly beans coming out. Cut the pointed end off and bend slightly. To attach the jelly bean funnel to the side of the ball cake, use a remnant of one of the dowels you have cut, push the dowel into the middle of the side of the ball, then push the funnel onto it, facing downwards. Attach the other funnel to the control centre on the opposite side of the cake in the same way, this time pointing upwards.

14 Colour 100g (3½oz) of White MMP with Berberis paste colour. Roll out half into a long sausage approximately 3mm (1/8") thick. Use the ribbon cutter to cut a thin ribbon approximately 5mm (1/8") wide. Wrap this around the base of the ball cake so it just touches the cake and attach using edible glue. Add some white vegetable fat to soften the rest of the paste, then extrude through the sugar shaper with the medium single-hole disc to make a string of paste. Use this string to decorate the ball cake: attach it around the mid section, on the top of the ribbon

of paste around the base of the ball, and around the top and bottom of the funnels.

15 Keep the paste in the shaper whilst you make the three coloured buttons on the front of the ball and the red button on the top of the ball. Make the balls from pinches of paste and colour using Fuchsia, Marigold and Gentian paste colours. Attach using edible glue then wrap a string of paste from the sugar shaper around each one. For the top button colour two pinches of paste with Fuchsia, attach in the same way, then add two strings of paste around the edge of the button and a third one stacked on top of these.

16 Make the three pipe coils from the aluminium wire: save a small amount for the glasses then cut the remaining wire into three sections, one long, one medium and one short. (You may find it easier to start with the shortest section first.) Colour approximately 25g (1oz) of MMP light Marigold for the short wire, 50g (1¾oz) Fuchsia for the medium wire and 75g (2½oz) Gentian for the long wire. Twist and

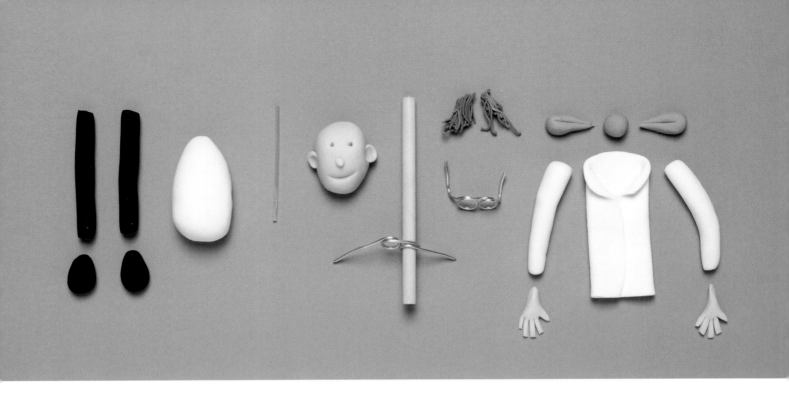

bend each wire into an interesting shape and hold it up to the cake to get an idea of where it will reach. Add a little white vegetable fat to the paste to make it more flexible and stop it cracking as you work. Roll the paste into a long sausage, making it thinner in sections and wider in others. Wrap it around the wire, approximately 1cm (³/₈") in from the end, securing it to itself with edible glue as you go. Stop when you get to 1cm (³/₈") from the end of the wire.

17 Hold the wire up against the cake and mark where the start and end of the wire will go into the cake with a flower veining tool. Insert a tiny posy pick into each of these points, push some of the remnant paste into the posy pick then push the wire end into the pick. Do this with all three wires.

18 Extrude more paste from the sugar shaper and wrap this around each of the wire ends to neaten the insertion points.

19 Take the remaining paste out of the sugar shaper and use five small pinches to shape the tiny buttons in front of the ball. Indent with the small end of the ball

tool as you attach them in place with edible glue.

20 Roll out the remnants of the Berberis paste and cut five discs using the end of the piping nozzle. Attach to the control centre. Thinly roll out a small amount of White MMP and cut five smaller circles using the micro circle cutter. Attach these on top of the Berberis discs. Use a craft knife to indent lines on the discs to resemble dials then paint with edible silver paint.

21 To make the mad professor, start with his shoes and legs. Take a pinch of Black SFP, make two cone shapes and flatten the points for the shoes. Roll the remainder into a long sausage using the cake smoother to make it even. Cut in half for the legs. Push a strand of spaghetti into the end of each leg and attach the shoes using edible glue. Stand them up to dry.

22 Once the legs are dry, shape 20g (³/₄oz) of White MMP into an egg shape. Attach to the top of the legs using strands of spaghetti and edible glue, then push a

strand through the top of the body ready to support the head. Allow the body to dry.

23 Colour 10g (just over ¼oz) of White MMP for the head with Chestnut paste colour. Pinch off a little for the ears and nose then shape the remainder into an oval and use the edge of a piping nozzle to mark a smile. Add a little ball of paste for the nose. Roll two tiny balls for the ears, attach to the head with a dot of edible glue, then indent the centre with the smaller end of the ball tool. Add two black eyes using tiny dots of Black MMP. Place the head on the body by pushing it onto the spaghetti strand and add a dab of edible glue to hold it in place.

24 Shape the remaining aluminium wire into the professor's glasses, using a piece of dowelling to get the frames the same size. Tuck the ends down the side of the face, by the ears.

IMPORTANT NOTE

Make sure the head and wire are both safely removed before the cake is served.

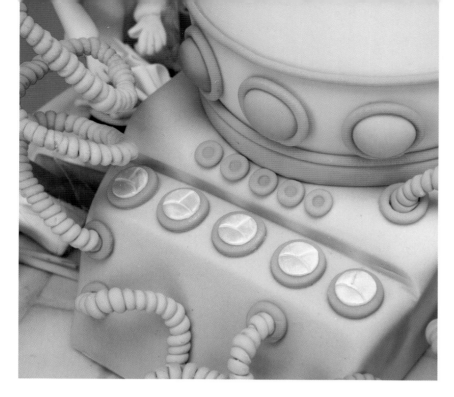

25 Make the hair by extruding the trimmings of Fuchsia coloured paste together with a small ball of Violet coloured MMP, both softened with white vegetable fat, through the sugar shaper with the multi-hole disc in position. Attach the hair to the head using edible glue. Cover the ends of the glasses with hair to help keep them in place.

26 Shape approximately 25g (1oz) of White MMP into a rectangle for the white coat. Measure around your figure to give you an idea of how long and wide the paste needs to be, cut it to size then wrap the paste around the body, using edible glue to secure it in place. Overlap the edges slightly at the front and turn back the top corners on each side to form the collar.

27 Make the two arms from 20g (just over ¾oz) of White MMP, roll into two sausages, flatten at one end for the shoulder and secure in place using edible glue. Bend at the elbow and hold in place with rolled up kitchen paper until dry.

28 Make two hands from a little White MMP coloured with Chestnut paste colour. Roll into two cones, flatten and mark the

fingers using the craft knife. Attach the hands to the sleeves using edible glue and a strand of spaghetti if required. Hold in place until dry.

29 Make a bowtie from remnants of Berberis paste: model two cone shapes and a ball for the centre and secure in place with edible glue. Position the mad professor on the cake drum.

30 Break the gelatine sheet into pieces and push it into the funnel on the left of the cake, allowing it to stick out of the funnel.

31 Using the remnants of paste, shape three green bottles. Roll any white paste very thinly and fold up several times to create a paper effect. Make an opened can by rolling some white paste into a short tube, wrap a thin rectangle of red paste around the tube for the label, then cut out a rough circle with the craft knife for the lid. Attach with edible glue then paint with edible silver paint. Make pipes of various colours by rolling paste into a sausage, cutting to the required length then indenting each end with the small end of a ball tool. Secure all the final pieces in place with edible glue.

shipwreck

Shiver me timbers!
This action-packed cake would
be perfect for budding seafarers
both young and old.

Edibles

25.5cm (10") heart shaped cake and 2
muffin-sized cupcakes (for the crow's nest)
300g (10½oz) buttercream
2kg (4lb 6½oz) sugarpaste: white
SK Mexican Modelling Paste (MMP): 150g
(5¼oz) Black, 300g (10½oz) White
SK Sugar Florist Paste (SFP): 20g (¾oz)
Black, 20g (¾oz) White
50g (1¾oz) SK Instant Mix Royal Icing
SK Paste Food Colours: Chestnut, Bulrush,
Jet Black, Marigold, Rose, Vine, Violet

Slices: approximately 48

SK Metallic Lustre Dust Food Colour:
Snowflake
SK Edible Metallic Paint: Gold
SK Piping Gel
White vegetable fat

Equipment

Basic equipment (see pages 6 to 9)
30.5cm (12") oval cake drum
22-gauge floral wires: white
7cm (2¾") circle cutter

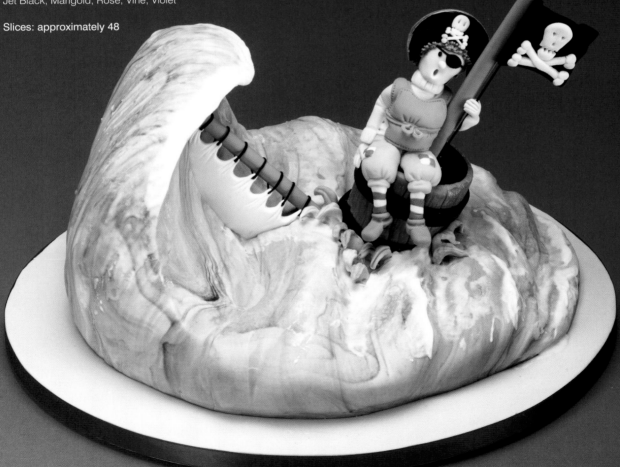

1 Cut the heart shaped cake in half horizontally using a small knife. Angle the knife upwards as you cut so the pointed end of the heart is thinner than the wide end: this end will form the support for the wave. Place the top part of the cake to one side.

2 Start cutting into the pointed end of the heart, shaping rough waves into the cake.

3 Cut the top half of cake in half lengthways: this part of the cake will form the large wave.

4 Stick these two pieces together with buttercream/jam, then use the small, sharp knife to cut the wave shape into the curved side of the cake.

5 Place the cake on top of the sea section and continue to trim the wave using the mini palette knife. Undercut the top of the cake slightly to create the curved wave shape.

6 Colour 500g (1lb 1½oz) of sugarpaste with Bluebell paste colour and blend well to achieve a uniform colour. Cover the cake drum using this paste and leave to dry.

7 Finish the tip of the wave using a pinch of sugarpaste as it is more stable than cake. Insert four or five strands of dried spaghetti into the wave to give it support, then attach the sugarpaste using a smear of buttercream to stick it to the cake. Build up the wave peaks using sausages of sugarpaste and smooth down either side to make a wave effect.

8 Cover the whole cake with buttercream then refrigerate until firm. When firm, transfer the cake to the prepared cake drum.

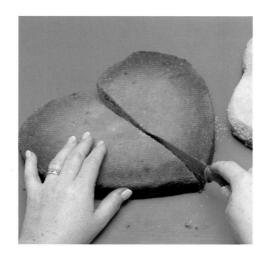
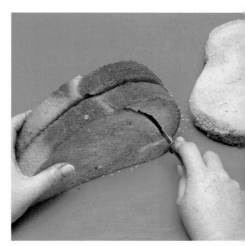

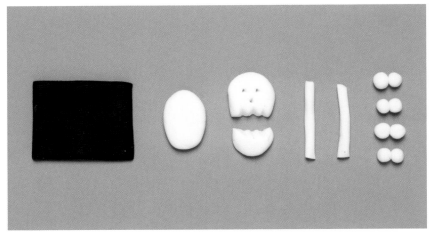

9 Cover the surface of the cake again with a light layer of buttercream to enable the sugarpaste to stick, making sure you don't get any buttercream on the covered drum.

10 Colour the remaining sugarpaste with Bluebell paste colour but don't blend the colour completely: leave streaks of light and dark paste to add to the effect. Roll out the paste and cover the wave cake, then work the paste into the mini waves using the flower shaping tool. Carefully work on the big wave, making sure you don't put too much pressure on the very tip of the wave. Trim around the excess paste carefully so as not to damage the covered cake drum and save the off-cuts of paste for later.

11 Make the crow's nest from the cupcakes by sticking one on top of the other with buttercream. Cover the surface with buttercream.

12 Roll out a small amount of Black MMP and cut a disc the same diameter as the top of the cake, i.e. approximately 7cm (2¾").

13 Colour 100g (3½oz) of White MMP with Bulrush to make a deep brown colour and roll out into a rectangle. Trim the lower edge straight using the pizza wheel, then wrap the paste around the stacked cupcakes. Trim the top flush with the top of the cake. Score the paste using the flower shaping tool to represent wooden planks.

14 Roll out a small amount of Black MMP and cut two strips using the ribbon cutter, each approximately 5mm (¹/₈") in width. Using edible glue, attach the strips widthways around the top and bottom of the crow's nest.

15 Take a cake dowel and brush edible glue three quarters of the way down the length. Roll out 50g (1¾oz) of dark brown modelling paste and cover the dowel where the glue is, leaving a quarter of the dowel exposed at the end. This is the mast.

16 Push the uncovered part of the dowel through the centre of the crow's nest, allowing it to go all the way through. Pick up the mast with the crow's nest attached, apply buttercream to the base of the crow's nest and position it on the

waves. Push the dowel down through the cake at an angle to help support the crow's nest on the cake.

17 Finish the crow's nest off by adding little waves around the base. Roll pinches of the blue sugarpaste remnants into teardrops, bend over the pointed end and attach in place using edible glue.

18 Cover the 22-gauge wire with black floral tape in preparation for the Jolly Roger.

19 To make the Jolly Roger, roll out some Black MMP and cut a 5cm (2") square. Make the skull and crossbones from White MMP by flattening an oval of paste and cutting three quarters of the way down to make a large and a small piece. Use the pointed end of the flower shaping tool to indent the teeth and eyes. Stick in place with edible glue. Cut two strands of white modelling paste for the crossbones and attach under the skull. Roll out eight tiny balls for the ends of the bones and attach two at each end with edible glue.

20 Attach the flag to the wire using edible glue, wrapping the edge of the paste around the wire. Leave to dry.

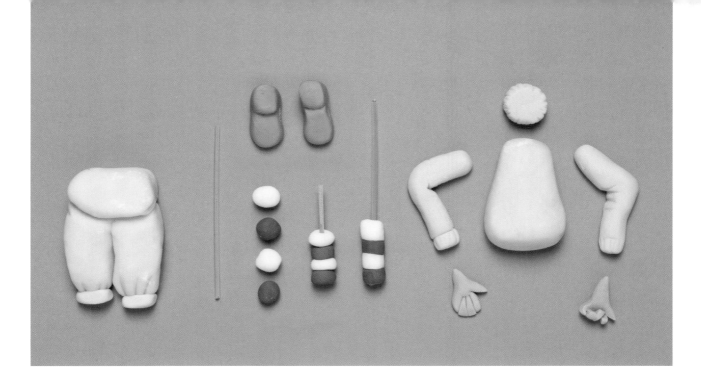

21 When the flag is dry, position it next to the mast and cut the wire level with the top of the crow's nest. Add a strip of Black MMP at the top of the mast and use edible glue at the other end to secure the wire to the mast.

22 Measure the length of dowel required for the sail mast (depending on the position of the wave it should be approximately 11cm/4¼"). Cover with paste in the same way as before. Push this into the cake at the base of the crow's nest so that the top of the mast doesn't quite touch the rising wave. Add small waves of blue sugarpaste at the base to cover up the point where the mast is inserted into the cake.

23 Make a template for the sail by holding a small piece of greaseproof paper against the cake and drawing on the angle of the mast and the curve of the wave. Cut it from 20g (¾oz) of White SFP, aiming to get the same curve as the wave so that it looks as if the sail is in the water. Use the pointed end of a flower shaping tool to add creases.

24 Place a little royal icing into a piping bag with a no. 1 nozzle. Attach the sail

in place by piping a slim trail of royal icing behind the edges, hold it in place then use a dry paintbrush to remove any excess icing.

25 Cut tiny strands of Black SFP to attach around the top of the mast and onto the sail. Again attach them in place with a little dot of royal icing.

26 Use the remaining royal icing to paint on the sea, adding white frothy tops to the waves. When dry, paint over the top with piping gel to give the waves and sea a watery look.

27 Make the pirate, starting with the trousers. Colour 50g (1¾oz) of White MMP with Vine paste colour. Shape into a short sausage then cut in half lengthways but only three quarters of the way up, leaving the legs attached at the top. Shape each leg, bend up the waist section and add creases using the flower shaping tool. Trim the ends of the legs to just below the knee, add some creases then attach a cuff made from a flattened ball of paste. Sit the trousers on the crow's nest.

28 Take a pinch of White MMP and colour with Violet paste colour. Make little balls of violet and white paste and push two of each

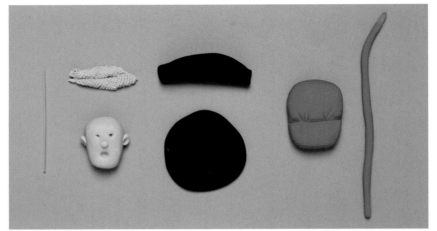

onto a strand of spaghetti. Roll slightly to smooth the surface then push the end of the spaghetti up into the trouser leg, using edible glue to secure it in place. Repeat on the other leg. Use remnants of the paste to make little patches on the trousers, again using two white and two violet balls squashed together. Secure with edible glue.

29 Colour 25g (1oz) of White MMP with Chestnut paste colour, cut in half then shape the shoes. Attach to the end of the stockings using edible glue. Save the remnants for the sailor's hair.

30 Make the jumper from 75g (2½oz) of White MMP coloured with a tiny amount of Marigold paste colour. Shape the body into a pear shape and attach in position leaning up against the mast. Shape two slim sausage shapes for the arms, indent the cuff and mark a ribbed effect using the flower shaping tool. Attach in place using edible glue. Wrap one arm firmly around the mast. Use the last of the paste to make the neck of the jumper, texture as before and attach with edible glue.

31 Make the hands and head from 50g (1¾oz) of White MMP coloured with a light dot of Chestnut to give a flesh colour. Pinch a small amount off this for ears, nose and hands. Shape the hands into a teardrop, cut the thumb and mark the fingers. Attach in place using edible glue.

32 Push a spaghetti strand down through the neck, body, trousers and into the crow's nest. Shape the head into an oval, indent the mouth using the small end of a ball tool, attach a tiny dot of paste for a nose and add two ears.

33 Make the hat from 25g (1oz) of Black MMP. Roll out the paste thickly and cut a circle using a 5cm (2") cutter. Roll the paste trimmings into a sausage, lay this across the centre of the circle, secure with edible glue, then draw the edges of the circle up together, again securing with edible glue. Indent the underside of the hat to make space for the head then attach to the head using royal icing, curving it around the head to the ears.

34 To make an eye patch from Black MMP, cut a fine strand and attach to the face using edible glue, then attach a small ball flattened over the eye socket. Use a tiny dot of paste for the other eye.

35 Use the remnants of paste from the shoes to make the hair. Add some white vegetable fat to the paste then extrude it through a sugar shaper fitted with the multi-hole disc to create lots of short strands of hair. Attach to the head with edible glue.

36 Make a skull and crossbones as before but make them smaller this time. Attach onto the hat.

37 Paint around the edge of the hat with edible gold paint and allow to dry.

38 Colour the remaining White MMP with Rose paste colour to make a deep pink for the life jacket. Remove a small amount and roll the remaining paste into a rough rectangle. Indent the middle using the flower shaping tool and add a crease. Indent the neck section and around the arms then use the stitching tool to texture the edges of the life jacket. Attach to the body with edible glue. Use the remaining paste to make a strap to go around the middle of the life jacket and attach with edible glue. Use the off-cuts from this to make a little bow in the middle.

venus fly trap

When I was designing this cake, I wanted to make something for the gardener that wasn't the usual plant pot, seed tray or watering can. This will definitely surprise the green-fingered gardener in your life!

Edibles

23cm (9") square cake

10cm (4") round cake

300g (10½oz) buttercream

3kg (6lb 9¾oz) sugarpaste: white

SK Mexican Modelling Paste (MMP): 50g
(1¾oz) Black, 600g (1lb 5¼oz) White

200g (7¼oz) SK Sugar Florist Paste (SFP):
White

30g (1oz) SK Instant Mix Royal Icing

SK Paste Food Colours: Holly/Ivy,
Hydrangea, Jet Black, Leaf Green,
Nasturtium, Rose, Vine, Terracotta

SK Dust Food Colours: Berberis, Bulrush,
Leaf Green, Vine

SK Metallic Lustre Dust Food Colour:
Snowflake

SK Pollen Style Dust Food Colour: Russet
or Semolina

White vegetable fat

Equipment

Basic equipment (see pages 6 to 9)

25.5m (10") round cake drum

1 pack 22-gauge floral wire (any colour)

Tiger Lily petal cutter: large (TT)

Casablanca Lily Petal Cutter: large (TT)

SK Great Impressions Veiners: Lily Petal
(Asiatic), Hosta Leaf

SK Great Impressions Teddy Bear Texture
Mat

2 small posy picks

Slices: approximately 38

1 Prepare the cake for the flowerpot first by trimming down the sides of the round cake, narrowing the base just like a plant pot. Once you are happy with the shape, wrap the cake in cling film to prevent it from drying out.

2 Carve the flower out of the square cake. Start by trimming away the corners, keeping as much width as possible.

3 Undercut the cake on one side to create the mouth of the flower. Don't cut off too much otherwise there is a risk that the cake may collapse. Keep all the offcuts of cake as you will need them to pad out the width and top of the cake. Trim around the cake further, taking off the corners and softening the edges.

4 Cover the top of the cake with a thin layer of buttercream and stick the off-cuts of cake onto the main cake to bulk out the shape further.

5 Cut and trim the cake to accentuate the mouth of the flower. Wrap in cling film as before until you are ready to cover the cake.

6 Prepare the cake drum by colouring 500g (1lb 1½oz) of white sugarpaste with a tiny dot of Holly/Ivy paste colour to give the paste a slight green tinge. Roll out and cover the cake drum in the usual way, then press the teddy texture mat onto the soft paste to indent the grass pattern. Leave to dry.

7 Colour 2.5kg (5lb 8¼oz) of sugarpaste with Vine paste colour for the flower cake. Cover the cake with buttercream first to allow the paste to stick to the cake, then roll out the sugarpaste and cover the cake. When placing the rolled out paste over the cake, take care not to break off the mouth of the flower by hanging heavy paste over it. Use your fingers to smooth the sugarpaste into the mouth, over and under it, keeping the opening wide. Smooth the rest of the paste around the cake and use a pad of paste in your fingers to polish the surface. Trim away the excess paste then tuck the edges under the cake to keep the curved shape of the flower. Leave to dry.

8 Once the cake is dry place it onto the prepared cake drum so the front edge of the cake is right up to the front edge of the drum, otherwise you will run out of space for the flowerpot.

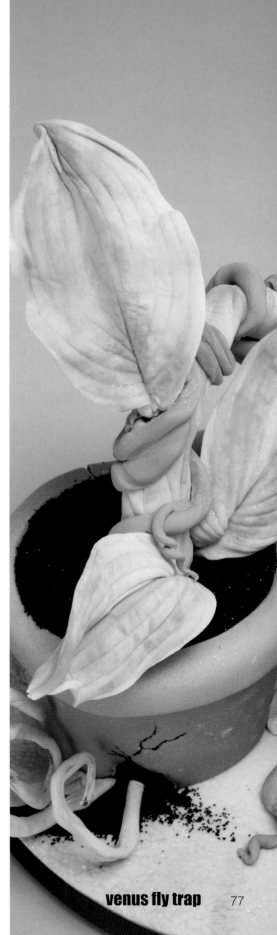

venus fly trap

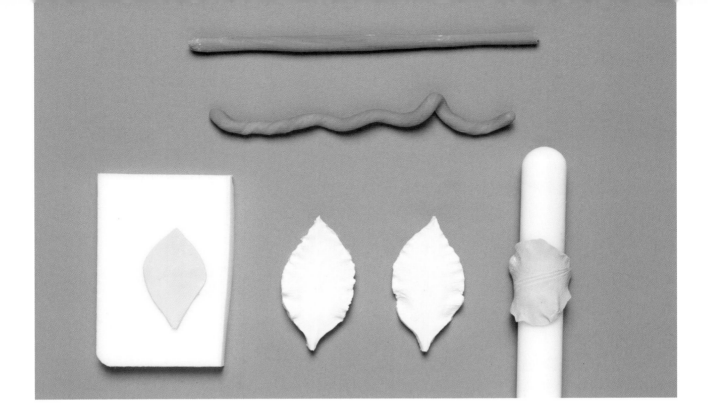

9 Colour 100g (3½oz) of White MMP with Rose paste colour to make a pale pink. Brush the inside of the mouth with edible glue, then line the mouth with the modelling paste and use the flower shaping tool to add little creases and indentations to the area. Knead together the remnants of the paste, deepen the colour then shape into a wavy tongue. Insert several spaghetti strands down the length of the tongue to give support, then insert this into the mouth.

10 Colour 50g (1¾oz) of White MMP with Hydrangea paste colour to make a pale blue shade. Roll out long, thin sausages of paste and attach around the mouth and up the sides of the flower using edible glue. Roll large and small balls from the remaining paste, flatten these in your palm and attach to the flower with edible glue. Brush the flower with a light dusting of Snowflake lustre dust to add a little sparkle.

11 Make the petals to go around the flower next. Colour 100g (3½oz) of SFP with Nasturtium paste colour to make

light orange. Roll out the paste thinly and cut out 12 petals with the Tiger Lily petal cutter. Vein the petals in the veiner then lay them over a rolling pin or similar shaped object to give a curved shape. They don't all have to be curved in exactly the same way: a variety of shapes will add interest to the design.

12 Once the petals are almost dry, dust with Berberis dust colour using a dry, flat paintbrush. Tap a little dust colour out of the pot onto a piece of kitchen roll, load the brush with dust, then knock off any excess before dusting the petals gently. Build up the colour gradually, making the centre darker if you wish. Once you are happy with the colour, do the same using the Snowflake dust to add sparkle.

13 Place a little royal icing into a piping bag with a no. 1 nozzle and attach the petals around the base of the flower with a dot of royal icing, framing the head.

14 Colour 1kg (2lb 3¼oz) of sugarpaste with the Terracotta paste colour. Fill and cover the flowerpot with buttercream then

roll out the paste and cover the pot. Use a pad of paste to smooth over the surface of the cake.

15 Use a craft knife to cut out a small, jagged section from the base of the pot. Extend the points of the section using the craft knife to resemble cracks.

TIP

It is difficult to make the back of the flowerpot neat but don't worry as it won't be seen. If you wish to cover the join you could use a strategically placed vine or leaf!

16 Fill the cracked section with the Black MMP, keeping the paste thinner than the pot edge. Paint the cracks with a little Jet Black paste colour using a very fine paintbrush.

17 Thickly roll out the remaining terracotta paste and use the ribbon cutter to cut out a band to go around the top of the pot. Attach with edible glue then smooth the top

edge of the band to soften the sharp edges. Position the pot onto the cake drum behind the flower.

18 Colour the remaining SFP with Leaf Green paste colour and cut out three or four leaves using a Casablanca Lily petal cutter. Insert a 22-gauge wire up through the centre of each leaf, then texture in the veiner. Curl and soften the edges of each leaf using the flower shaping tool on a foam pad. Leave to dry. Dust the leaves with Leaf Green dust colour in the same way as for the petals.

19 Colour the remaining SFP a darker shade of Leaf Green and put to one side, sealed in a polythene bag to prevent it from drying out.

20 Take the remaining MMP and colour it light green using Leaf Green paste colour. Shape the paste into a long, wide sausage to make the flower stem. Draw lines down the stem with the pointed end of the flower shaping tool, coiling the lines around the paste to give a twisted appearance.

21 Cut six 22-gauge wires to approximately 15cm (6") in length, tape

together with floral tape and insert this into a posy pick. Push the pick into the centre of the flowerpot. Push the end of the green stem onto the wire and coil the rest of the sausage around the back of the flower. Re-texture with the flower shaping tool.

22 Use the darker green SFP reserved from earlier and roll into a long, thin sausage. Bind this around the flower stem and onto the cake drum to resemble a vine sucker. Insert the leaves into the stem, cutting the wires to the required length as you do so.

23 Roll the remnants of paste into sausage shapes approximately 10cm (4") long. Insert a 22-gauge wire approximately 12cm (5") long into each sausage, coil the wire to create the curled roots and insert into a posy pick, then push this into the hole in the base of the pot.

24 Colour some Russet pollen dust or semolina with Bulrush dust colour to make it dark brown. Brush the top of the plant pot and the hole in the pot with edible glue, then sprinkle the pollen dust or semolina over to represent soil.

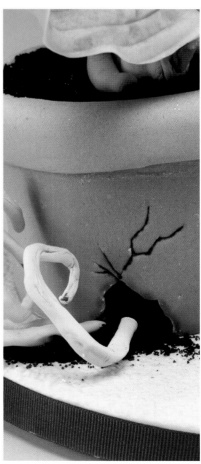

wizard

Edibles

25.5cm (10") square cake

250g (8¾oz) buttercream

Sugarpaste: 2kg (4lb 6½oz) black, 3kg
(6lb 9¾oz) white

400g (14½oz) SK Mexican Modelling Paste
(MMP): Black

SK Paste Food Colours: Berberis, Bluebell,
Bulrush, Chestnut, Jet Black, Vine, Violet

SK Dust Food Colours: Berberis, Rose

SK Metallic Lustre Dust Food Colour: Light
Gold

SK Edible Metallic Paint: Gold, Silver

SK Edible Glue

Equipment

Basic equipment (see pages 6 to 9)

Stained glass texture mat (SA)

23cm (9") square cake drum

Small star cutter

Floral wire: silver

Slices: approximately 45

This is a really easy cake to make but looks quite impressive. It would be perfect for any budding wizards in the family!

1 Colour 500g (1lb 1½oz) of white sugarpaste grey using Jet Black paste colour. Roll out the paste and cover the cake drum. Save the remnants for later to make bindings for the books.

2 Start by cutting out the rectangular cakes in various sizes. You will need five cakes in total, each one different in size, so use a long, sharp knife and a ruler to carve each one. For the largest book, cut out a block measuring 15cm x 10cm x 7.5cm (6" x 4" x 3") from one corner of the cake.

3 Cut another piece below the first measuring 7.5cm x 7.5cm x 3.5cm (3" x 3" x 1½").

4 Cut a third book next to the second measuring 5cm x 7.5cm x 3cm (2" x 3" x 1½").

5 Trim off the outer crust from the side of the cake and cut the next book out of the cake to measure 5cm x 7.5cm x 2.5cm (2" x 3" x 1").

6 Cut the final book out of the remaining cake measuring 7.5cm x 9cm x 5cm (3" x 3½" x 2").

7 Cut off any brown crusts from the cakes then trim the edges off the books using a mini palette knife. Work your way around each book in turn, shaping each edge away. Wrap any books you are not working on in cling film to stop them drying out and place in the fridge to keep them cool.

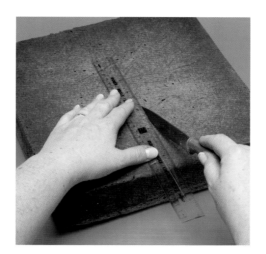

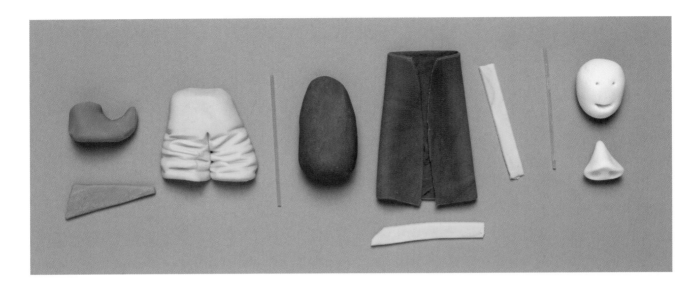

8 Cover the cakes with a thin layer of buttercream and then cover with a thin layer of white sugarpaste. You will need approximately 1kg (2lb 3¼oz) of sugarpaste for all the cakes. This will keep the crumbs at bay and will seal the cakes to keep them moist. Allow to dry before moving to the next step.

9 All the books are covered in the same way so follow the same instructions to cover each book. Cover the cakes with another thin layer of white sugarpaste, sticking it to the previous one using a little cooled, boiled water. Smooth the paste over the book and use the flower veining tool to mark the pages by scoring along three sides of the book.

10 Once the books are dry, dust the pages with Light Gold lustre dust to pick out the page edges.

11 Make the binding for the books by rolling out approximately 1kg (2lb 3¼oz) for the largest book and 400g–600g (14¼oz–1lb 5¼oz) for the smaller books. Roll out the paste to form a rough rectangle, dampen the book to be bound with cooled, boiled water then place the book to one side of the paste, leaving a border around the edge. Fold the book over to the opposite side, then use the pizza wheel to trim away any excess paste. Do this for all the books. To emboss a pattern onto two of the book covers, put the book onto the texture mat whilst the paste is still soft and press firmly.

12 To add lettering to some of the books, colour a small piece of MMP with Daffodil paste colour, use a craft knife to cut long, narrow strips and arrange them to spell out 'spell book'.

TIP

You could change the wording on the book covers to personalise the cake for the occasion.

13 Make the wizard, starting with the boots. Colour 25g (1oz) of MMP with Bulrush paste colour and shape into two

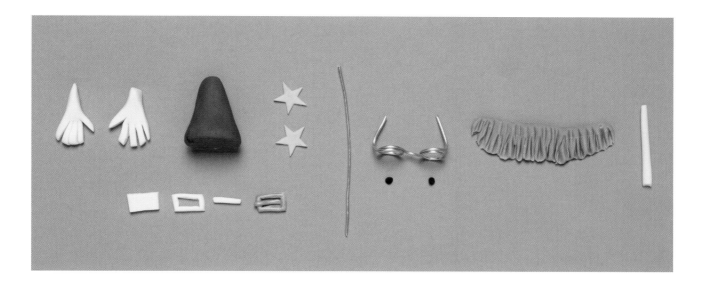

boots with the toes turned up. Colour 20g (¾oz) of MMP with Chestnut paste colour and use half the paste to make the soles of the boots. Roll into two triangles and attach to the base of the boots with edible glue. Roll out the other 10g (¼oz) of Chestnut paste to make boot tops and cut two triangles to wrap around the top of the boots. Add a little white vegetable fat to the remnants of Chestnut paste and extrude a single string of paste using the sugar shaper. Attach this around the boots where the sole meets the boot. Add a buckle to the boots by cutting a remnant of paste (black if you wish) into a tiny rectangle, then use a craft knife to cut out the middle of the buckle. Attach with edible glue and paint with edible silver paint. Leave to dry.

14 Shape the trousers from 50g (1¾oz) of White MMP coloured with Vine paste colour. Make a rectangle, make a small cut up the middle, soften the edges and add creases to the front of the trousers with the flower veining tool. Attach the boots to the trousers using edible glue and a spaghetti strand.

15 Make the body from 50g (1¾oz) of MMP coloured with Violet paste colour. Shape into an egg with the pointed end being the neck of the wizard. Attach this to the trousers with edible glue and spaghetti strands. Colour 25g (1oz) of MMP with Vine paste colour and use the ribbon cutter to cut thin strips of paste. Run two ribbons down the front of the body and a ribbon at right angles across the base of the body to make a short coat. Make a black belt in the same way using a pinch of Black MMP and attach all the ribbons in place with edible glue. Add a little buckle, made in the same way as before.

16 Roll out a cloak for the wizard from 75g (2½oz) Violet coloured MMP, cut into a rectangle with the pizza wheel and wrap around the wizard, allowing it to billow out at the front. Attach with edible glue then trim with Vine coloured paste ribbons as before.

17 Colour 55g (2oz) of White MMP with a hint of Chestnut paste colour to make a flesh colour. Use 25g (1oz) for the hands, roll into two teardrop shapes, mark fingers

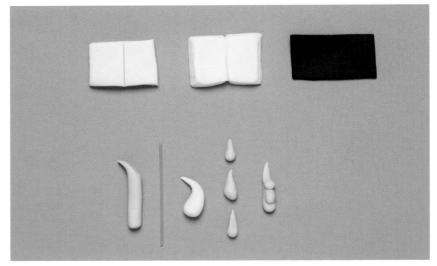

and elongate the wrists. Make a little book as before to go into one hand and attach with edible glue. Cut a strip of paste from any remnants to make the wand and attach this to the other hand with edible glue. Wrap the fingers around each item then attach the hands to the body by tucking the elongated wrist between the side of the body and the cape. Support in position until dry.

18 Make the head from 30g (1oz) of the flesh coloured paste. Shape a large nose from this paste then roll a ball for the head and attach to the body using edible glue and a spaghetti strand (the head is quite heavy so will need this support). Shape a hat from 15g (½oz) of Violet coloured MMP and attach to the head using edible glue. Add little Vine coloured stars to the hat and trim with Vine coloured ribbons of paste as before.

19 Make the wizard's glasses from a piece of silver floral wire. Shape into two small circles next to each other and attach to the face by pushing the wire

ends into the head of the wizard. Add two dots of Black MMP for the eyes.

20 To make the hair, colour 25g (1oz) of White MMP with a tiny dot of Jet Black paste colour. Shape the paste into sections, making the beard and moustache first. Texture the paste using the flower veining tool and attach to the face using edible glue. Work your way around the wizard's head, making sections of hair and texturing as described above.

21 Make little books in the same way as the big ones but rather than using cake, model small rectangles of paste, approximately 15g (½oz).

22 Shape the candles from pinches of paste rolled into sausages and insert a spaghetti strand through the sausage. Make a little flame by rolling a pinch of coloured paste into a teardrop shape and attach onto the top of the spaghetti strand with edible glue. Paint the flames using a mixture of lustre dust and clear alcohol. I painted the ones around the wizard blue and the ones further away red. Paint the deep colour first, leave to dry then paint the lighter orange/gold or blue/silver over the top. Make the drips of wax by rolling pinches of paste into teardrops and attaching to the side of the candle with edible glue. Secure the candles to the cake.

23 Finish the cake by making potion bottles from 15g (½oz) of MMP, or less depending on the size of the bottle. Roll into a teardrop then flatten the pointed end to make a bottle top. Secure to the cake and board, filling in any gaps between the books.

mini books

These little spell books are easy to make using mini squares of cake, either baked in a mini cake pan or carved from a large, square cake. Fill and cover the cakes in the same way as the big books, then pipe the names of your party guests with white royal icing and a no. 1.5 piping nozzle.

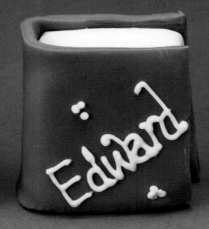

safari sunset

I've always wanted to go on a safari but have never been lucky enough – this is the closest I have got to photographing big game!

Edibles

25.5cm (10") square sponge cake

260g (9oz) buttercream

Sugarpaste: 1kg (2lb 3¼oz) black, 4kg (8lb 13oz) white

400g (14¼oz) SK Mexican Modelling Paste (MMP): White

500g (1lb 1½oz) SK Sugar Florist Paste (SFP): White

250g (8¾oz) SK Instant Mix Royal Icing

SK Paste Food Colours: Berberis, Chestnut, Fern, Fuchsia, Gentian, Jet Black, Leaf Green, Violet

SK Dust Food Colour: Berberis

SK Metallic Lustre Dust Food Colours: Antique Gold, Light Gold

Clear alcohol (e.g. gin or vodka)

Cornflour duster

Equipment

Basic equipment (see pages 6 to 9)

30.5cm x 35.5cm (12" x 14") rectangular cake drum

25.5cm x 30.5cm x (10" x 12") oval cake drum

2 x 25.5cm x 30.5cm x (10" x 12") oval cake dummies

Thin, food-grade card (e.g. a cereal box)

Sticky tape

SK Great Impressions Wheel Mould: large

Heated craft pen (optional)

Low tack tape (e.g. masking tape)

Safari frieze template (see page 95)

Off-road vehicle templates (see page 95)

Slices: approximately 45

1 Attach the two cake dummies together to make a large oval, turn it on its side and wedge it into a box or bowl to keep it in this position. Cover the side with a sheet of thin card and tape down with sticky tape to make a smooth surface. Dust with cornflour. This will be the former for the backdrop.

2 Colour all the White SFP light gold with Berberis paste colour. Roll out smoothly to around 3mm (⅛") thick and cut out a 44.5cm x 10cm (17½" x 4") rectangle. Round off the top edge to create the backdrop for the safari scene.

3 Lay the SFP over the prepared former to dry. Once dry, lift it off carefully and stand it up on the flat side, then leave to dry completely for 24 hours. Dust off the cornflour with a dry brush.

4 Prepare the base drums by sticking the oval drum centrally on top of the rectangular drum with a little royal icing. Roll out the black sugarpaste and cover the oval drum first, then cover the exposed area on the rectangular drum. Smooth with cake smoothers and a pad of paste.

5 Place the backdrop up against the edge of the oval drum. Use dots of royal icing to secure it to the side of the oval drum and press it into the soft black sugarpaste for added support.

6 Colour 20g (just under ¾oz) of White MMP with Berberis paste colour. Add some white vegetable fat to soften the paste then extrude through the sugar shaper fitted with the small hole disc to give you a long string of paste. Attach this along the top edge of the backdrop using edible glue. Leave to dry.

7 Once dry, attach gold ribbon to the edge of the oval drum (see page 24). Allow this to go all the way around, including around the back of the backdrop. This will secure the backdrop further.

8 Prepare the template to stencil the backdrop. Take the acetate and place the template for the trees and giraffes underneath, approximately 1cm (⅜") from the edge of the acetate. If you are using a heated craft pen, place the

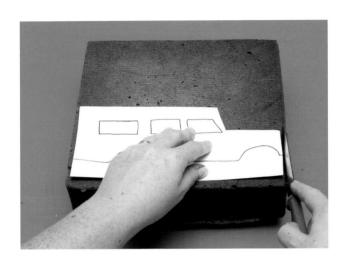 

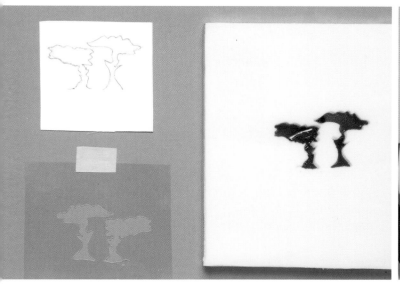

template and acetate onto a heatproof work surface and cut out the stencil design from the acetate.

TIP

If you don't have a heated pen you could use a craft knife to cut out the design instead.

9 Place the stencil up against the backdrop and secure with some low tack tape. Colour the remaining royal icing with Jet Black paste colour then use a small palette knife to scrape the black royal icing over the stencil smoothly and firmly.

10 Repeat this several times to build up the scene across the backdrop. Each time you remove the stencil, wipe it clean with a damp cloth before re-attaching it further along. Leave to dry.

11 Finish the backdrop by adding in a ribbon of black sugarpaste along the base of the stencilled shapes to neaten the base. To make this, thinly roll the black sugarpaste and use a ribbon cutter to cut a long strip approximately 1cm ($^3/_8$") wide. Secure to the base of the backdrop with edible glue, then make tiny tufts of grass and attach along the top of the ribbon with edible glue.

12 To finish the scene, use the Light Gold, Berberis and Antique Gold dust colours to dust the backdrop, giving the effect of the setting sun.

TIP

Mask the cake drum under the backdrop with kitchen towel to prevent the dust colour from getting all over the black paste.

13 To carve the car from the cake, first make templates for your chosen car (see further details in the Microcar project, page 34). If you are using a different template to the one provided, make sure the shape you have chosen is no bigger than half the length of the cake. Place the template up against the lower half of the cake and pin in place using glass-headed pins or cocktail sticks if preferred.

14 Take a long, sharp knife and start cutting around your template, making sure you don't undercut the shape.

15 Place the cut cake on top of the other half cake and cut the shape again.

16 Stick both sides together with a thin layer of buttercream.

17 Place the template back up against the cake sides and cut out the wheel arches with a mini palette knife. Use the same tool to mark any defining lines on the body work and the windows.

18 Cut out the cake from under the wheel arches and where the wheels will be, using the template as a guide. Don't trim too far into the base of the cake as you need sufficient cake underneath to support it.

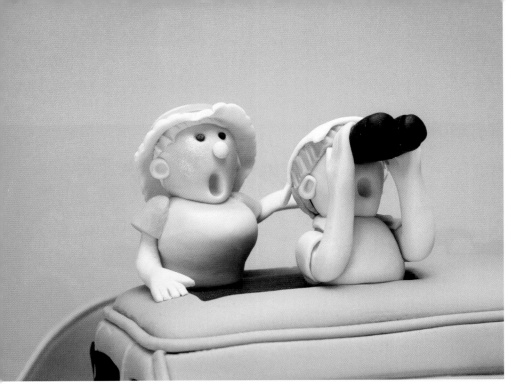

19 Use the mini palette knife to trim the edges of the car, creating the curved shape. Work your way around the car, trimming off any sharp corners to soften the whole shape.

20 Cover the cake with a thin layer of buttercream, then cover with 500g (1lb 1½oz) of white sugarpaste. Roll the paste quite thinly and smooth it into the shape of the cake to give you a smooth working surface. Whilst the paste is still soft, use the pointed end of a flower veining tool to mark the paste with guidelines for the sections of the car. You can either use the templates provided or make your own and you can mark as much or as little you want to aid your decorating. Make sure you mark the front of the car and take a template of the bonnet so you can re-create it in green paste.

21 Roll approximately 200g (7¼oz) of Black MMP into a thin strip and run this around the base of the cake. The strip needs to be as deep as the wheel arches and should be rolled thinly to cover the base of the cake under the bumper and in the wheel arches.

22 Colour 1.2kg (2lb 10¼oz) of white sugarpaste with Leaf Green paste colour. Seal any paste you aren't using in a plastic bag to stop it drying out.

TIP

It is best to colour all the paste you need now so the car is the same colour all over.

23 If you are using the templates provided, you may need to enlarge them to the size you want for your cake. Cut the sections of the car starting with the long side section, using approximately 400g (14¼oz) of paste. Cut the green sections reasonably thick so the markings can be applied and to give the car a chunky feel. Secure the bodywork in place with edible glue, then use a pad of paste to smooth the surface. Trim around the wheel arch and neaten.

24 Mark the doors and use the flower veining tool and a ruler to indent distinct lines around the doors and windows.

25 Cut out the windows and replace with Black MMP. Add little strips of paste for door handles.

26 Roll out approximately 25g (1oz) of the green paste quite thickly for the wheel arches. Cut two, one for the front and one for the back wheel. Secure to the car with edible glue. Repeat the whole process on the other side of the car.

27 Cover the back of the car next with 100g (3½oz) of green sugarpaste. Attach as before, indent with the flower veining tool and add black sugarpaste windows.

28 Cover the front of the car next. Roll out a rectangle from approximately 90g (3oz) of green paste and cover the windscreen area. Cut out the windscreen and replace with a strip of black sugarpaste.

29 Roll out 100g (3½oz) of green paste for the bonnet and attach to the front of the car. Butt the paste up against the window, carefully trim each side and smooth neatly round the side of the bonnet.

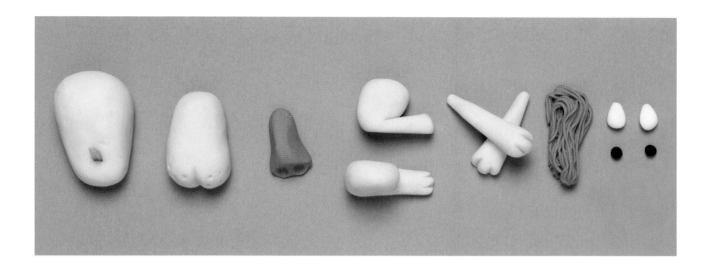

30 Take a rough template of the bonnet and trim this on both sides to create the raised bonnet section that the lion will sit on. Attach this in the same way then use the flower veining tool to scribe the lines of the front grille.

31 Cut two squares for headlights from two pinches of green paste.

32 Roll the remnants of black sugarpaste into a sausage, flatten and cut a long ribbon using the ribbon cutter. Attach to the front and back of the car for bumpers.

33 Using approximately 50g (2oz) of Black MMP for each wheel, make five wheels using the mould and attach in place using edible glue.

34 Make a template for the roof section. Roll out approximately 75g (2½oz) of green sugarpaste, place the template on top and cut around it using a pizza wheel. Use the craft knife to mark the sunroof, then remove the template and finish cutting the sunroof out, making it as neat as you can. Don't take too long over this as the paste will be drying as you

work. Attach to the car using edible glue and smooth the join between the roof and the side pieces. Fill in the sunroof with a square of black sugarpaste.

35 Colour 25g (1oz) of White MMP with Leaf Green paste colour, add a little white vegetable fat then extrude through the sugar shaper with the single-hole disc to create a long, thin string of paste. Use this string to neaten the join around the roof.

36 All of the figures are made from MMP. For the lion, colour 50g (1¾oz) of paste to a light cream with a little Berberis paste colour. Form the body into an egg shape and insert two spaghetti strands into the narrower end to support the head. Make the front paws from two pinches of paste, attach to the body and cross one over the other. Shape the back legs from 10g (¼oz) and attach with edible glue. Make the head next from approximately 20g (just under ¾oz) and form into an egg shape. Mark the mouth and attach in place using edible glue. Colour the remaining paste a deeper brown using a dot of Chestnut paste colour. Pinch off a little for the nose then soften the rest with white vegetable

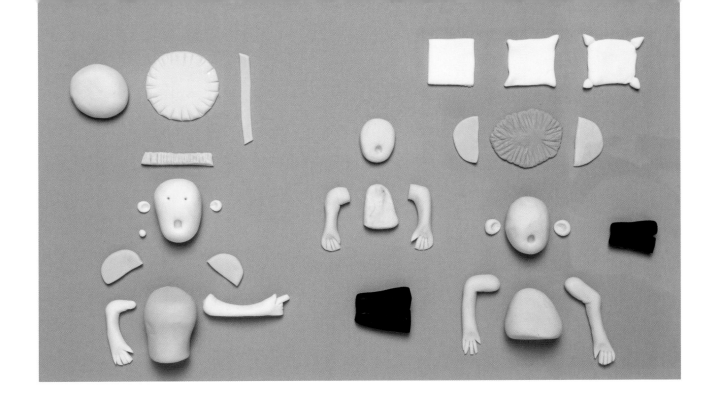

fat and extrude through the sugar shaper using the multi-hole disc. Attach the mane to the head with edible glue. Add in the eyes made from two tiny pinches of white paste rolled into teardrops and add in two tiny dots of black paste for pupils. Position the lion on the bonnet of the car.

37 The figures are made of all the same body parts: two arms, a body, a head, hair, a hat and binoculars (except for the woman pointing at the lion, she's the only one who's spotted it!). Colour the MMP for the shirts as follows: 25g (1oz) pale Fuchsia, 15g (½oz) pale Gentian and a pinch of pale Violet. For the man and woman, pinch out a little paste to make the sleeves and shape the rest into the body. Attach all the bodies to the car using edible glue. Shape the heads and add small balls for the nose and ears. Mark each mouth with a flower veining tool. Add two tiny black eyes for the woman (the other two have binoculars). All the arms are made the same way by rolling a sausage using approximately 10g (¼oz) of paste, cutting to the required length, flattening one end for the hand and attaching the other end to the body. Add short sleeves to the top two figures. Add hair and hats as required and secure everything in place with edible glue.

templates

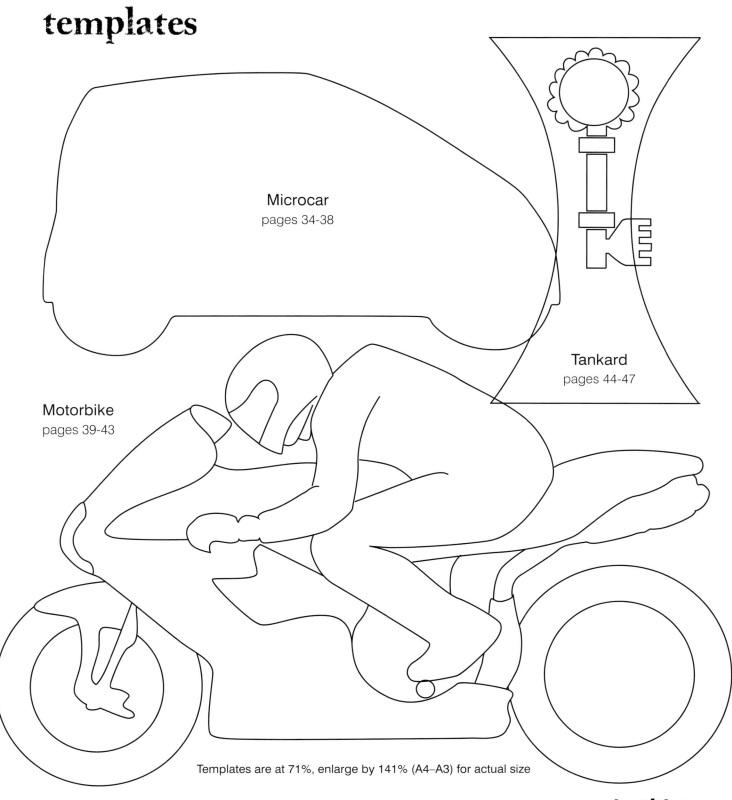

Microcar
pages 34-38

Tankard
pages 44-47

Motorbike
pages 39-43

Templates are at 71%, enlarge by 141% (A4–A3) for actual size

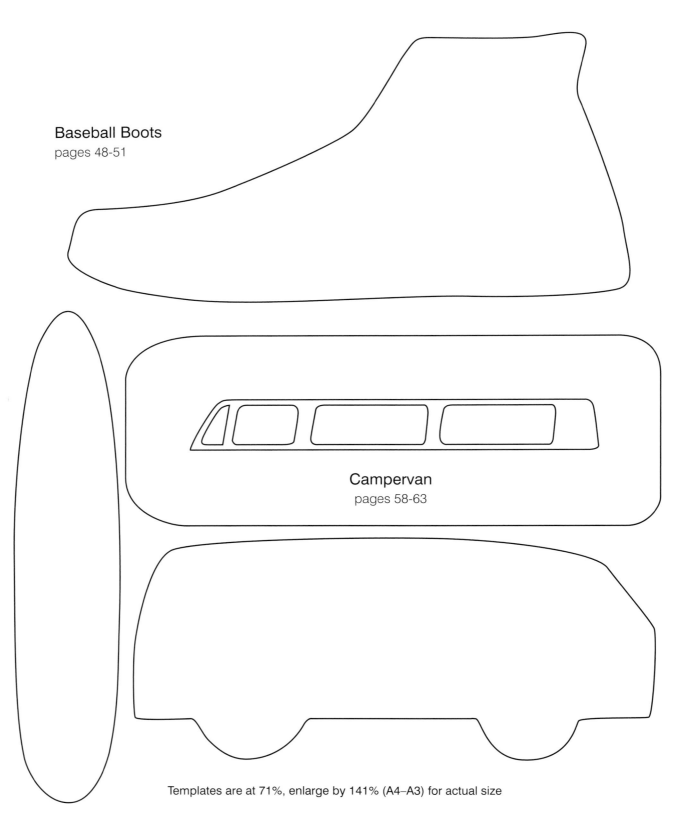

Baseball Boots
pages 48-51

Campervan
pages 58-63

Templates are at 71%, enlarge by 141% (A4–A3) for actual size

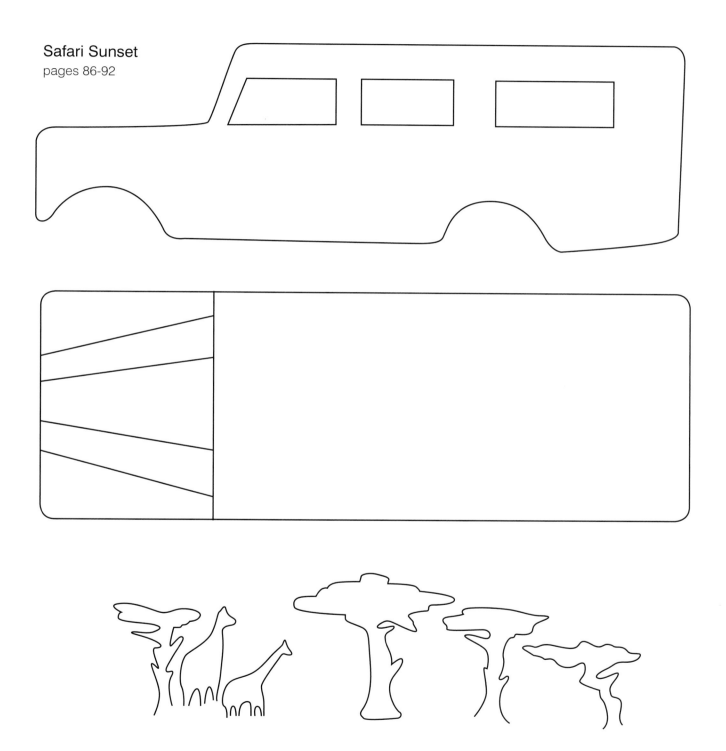

Safari Sunset

pages 86-92

Templates are at 71%, enlarge by 141% (A4–A3) for actual size

Squires Kitchen, UK

3 Waverley Lane
Farnham
Surrey
GU9 8BB
0845 61 71 810
+44 1252 260 260
www.squires-shop.com

Squires Kitchen International School

The Grange
Hones Yard
Farnham
Surrey
GU9 8BB
0845 61 71 812
+44 1252 260 262
www.squires-school.co.uk

Squires Kitchen, France

+33 (0) 1 82 88 01 66
clientele@squires-shop.fr
www.squires-shop.fr

Squires Kitchen, Italy

www.squires-shop.it

Squires Kitchen, Spain

+34 93 180 7382
cliente@squires-shop.es
www.squires-shop.es

suppliers

SK stockists

Jane Asher Party Cakes
London
020 7584 6177

Blue Ribbons
Surrey
020 8941 1591

Think Cake
Kent
01622 695627

Lawsons Ltd.
Devon
01752 892543

The Sugarcraft Emporium
Worcestershire
01527 576703

Surbiton Art & Sugarcraft
Surrey
020 8391 4664

SK distributors

UK

Confectionery Supplies
Herefordshire
www.confectionerysupplies.co.uk

Guy Paul & Co. Ltd.
Buckinghamshire
www.guypaul.co.uk

Culpitt Ltd.
Northumberland
www.culpitt.com

Australia & New Zealand

Zoratto Enterprises
New South Wales
+61 (2) 9457 0009

Manufacturers

FMM Sugarcraft
Hertfordshire
www.fmmsugarcraft.com

Kit Box
North Somerset
www.kitbox.co.uk

Knightsbridge PME Ltd.
London
www.cakedecoration.co.uk

Lindy's Cakes
Buckinghamshire
www.lindyscakes.co.uk

Orchard Cake Tools
Netherlands
www.orchardcaketools.com

Patchwork Cutters
Merseyside
www.patchworkcutters.com

Smeg UK Ltd.
www.smeguk.com
www.smegretro.co.uk
Italian appliance manufacturer Smeg
produces distinctive domestic appliances
combining design, performance and
quality.

Sugar Artistry Ltd.
Wiltshire
www.sugar-artistry.co.uk